DATE DUE

MR 17'98			
AP 23'98			
JA 23'01			
DE 18 03			
AP 23 04			

DEMCO 38-296

all about beads

all about beads

a guide to beads and bead jewellery making

Maureen Murray

B T Batsford Ltd · London

R

Acknowledgements

I would like to thank our Indian bead suppliers for their assistance and also their beadmakers for allowing me to take photographs, especially Mr O. P. Gupta, Mr R. K. Gupta, Mr V. K. Gupta, Mr R. Tandon and Mr Mustaq. I am also grateful to our suppliers of Czechoslovakian beads (Mr H. Henrey) and Peruvian beads (Mo Fini), Janice Farley of Connecticut for information about porcelain beads, Frank Murray for information about ceramic glazes, Edward Schwalbe for information about plastic beads and English glass beadmaker Bill Tuffnell.

I would like especially to thank Nancy Wall of Beadworks, Connecticut for the loan of many beads from her collection and my colleagues at the Covent Garden Bead Shop, Serah Pope, Ursula Geisselmann and Sarah Healy for their support and help with the design and making up of jewellery pieces, particularly Charlotte Smith for checking my instructions.

I would also like to thank Andy Cameron for his superb photography, Garry Mouat for his help and for lending his Ethiopian cross and rudraksha beads and Rob Lamb for designing such a stunning book. I would particularly like to thank my editor Venetia Penfold for her enthusiasm, encouragement and unfailing good humour and patience in organizing this project.

First published 1995

© J.R.M. Beads and Maureen Murray

ISBN 0 7134 7863 2

A catalogue record for this book is available from the British Library.

Published by
B.T. Batsford Ltd
4 Fitzhardinge Street
London W1H OAH

Printed in Hong Kong

Photographs by Andy Cameron

Illustrations by Sibylla Duffy and Anthony Lawrence

Contents

Introduction 6

About Beads

Techniques

Projects

Introduction

Since the beginning of history, wherever there is evidence of man's existence, beads have been discovered. They range from the simplest pierced shells and seeds to the beautifully carved and intricately worked precious materials. In all cultures their function has been not merely to provide decoration but also to indicate wealth or status. They form a significant part in religious or ceremonial rituals and have been used as good luck charms and to give protection from malign influence. Throughout the ages, beads have played a significant role in the exchange of commodities – as late as the nineteenth century, fine glass beads made in Europe were bartered for furs, ivory, gold and even slaves.

Our English word 'bead' comes from the old English 'gebed' meaning 'prayer', probably because of its association with the Catholic rosary, a chain or string of beads, used as an aid to prayer and meditation. In most major world religions, some form of rosary is used to symbolize and count prayers made to the deity.

The word 'bead' usually signifies in most people's minds a small spherical object with a hole running through it. In fact, any object, pierced or grooved for stringing and small enough to be worn on the person could be termed a bead.

Today the variety of shapes and materials used for beads is endless, and there are now means of mass-producing an infinite range in complex, subtle shapes and colours. However, many of the most beautiful are still being made using ancient traditional techniques.

The first part of this book will provide the enthusiast with information about beads, how they are made and some of the history and folklore which surrounds them. The second section aims to show those with a creative flair how beads are used to make all kinds of jewellery. The third section consists of a number of projects of varying degrees of complexity to provide a starting point. They are intended to provide inspiration and a guide to designing jewellery. Whilst the beads and findings used should be readily available from most suppliers, they can be substituted with similar beads of different colours or materials.

about beads

chapter one

Natural Materials

Top Loose beads, carved or natural seeds, carved bamboo segment, drilled giant sea-urchin spine (centre), dentalia shell (tusk-like), abalone chip, blue Paua shell pendant, amber nugget (top left). The brown and white patterned beads are 'pumtek' – petrified wood, copies of ancient Burmese sacred beads. Strings: white heishi discs (ostrich shell), small rudraksha (Hindu sacred beads), tiny snail shells, shell beads stained coral-pink and drilled branches of white coral

The earliest 'beads' were shells, fossils, seeds, stones and animal and fish vertebrae threaded with animal sinews or vegetable fibres through their natural perforations. Excavations of ancient burial grounds and cave paintings dating from about 30,000 BC produce evidence of necklaces and pendants made from these types of beads. They were worn not only as trophies and for personal adornment but also in the belief that the hunter would acquire the strength of the slain creature and in some magical way be protected from it. Later these materials were chipped into shape with sharpened flakes of flint stone.

Once metals had been mined, they began to be fashioned into tools so that more sophisticated work became possible. Metal was drawn into wire and used for threading beads of worked stone, amber, ivory and bone.

Mining for precious metals brought the incidental discovery of coloured crystals and rocks with mysterious markings. These were cut, polished and set in precious metal or drilled to be made into beads. In what seemed like magic, sparkling gemstones emerged from the rough earth, and dull stones and pebbles were transformed into beautiful jewels. The wearing of these symbolized wealth and status and was believed to protect against evil and cure illness. Certain gems could only be cut with diamond chips bound to an iron tool and pierced with drills using diamond dust mixed with oil as a lubricant. These laborious hand methods have now largely been replaced with high speed, ultra-fine, diamond-tipped drills which pierce the stone accurately.

Bone

Because of the growing awareness of the cruelty to animals in the ivory trade, bone carving has replaced the traditional craft of ivory carving. After cleaning and bleaching the bone, it is then cut and polished into shape. It is often stained by boiling in tea to imitate old ivory. Vegetable or chemical dyes are also used to stain bone or horn with bright or subtle colours, either before or after carving – very attractive effects are obtained by staining the surface, then carving it to show the white below.

Most beads of natural material are carved now with power-assisted lathes and drills, but the ancient bow drill is still in use. Significant quantities of bone beads are formed in India like this – the operator grips a piercing tool between his toes while the bead is held in a 'chuck' wound with the string of the bow; as the bow is moved backwards and forwards the bead is turned to and fro, thus enabling it to be pierced, or grooved with a design.

African carving is rather more primitive than the Indian methods but the Africans have perfected a particularly successful type of bone decoration with the 'batik' process. Melted wax is trailed in a design onto the surface before dyeing the bead – it is then removed by heating, leaving the design in white.

Horn

Horn is another natural material used to make beads. It is softened by boiling, then moulded, ground or carved into shape. Horn can be polished, keeping the natural colour but can also be bleached or stained to resemble amber and wood.

Above Indian beadmaker using a bow drill to make bone beads

Above left Bone and horn beads which include a bone bird fetish, bone and horn pipe beads, bleached white and black Indian bone beads, African black and white 'batik' beads, carved Chinese, smoked bone and red-stained amber beads

Left Wooden beads and pendants which include: polished and carved or brass inlaid ebony and rosewod from India, African carved ebony tusk and comb head pendant, large round rose-wood and sheesham wood bead, Chinese carved cinnabar and black-stained lacquer beads

Wood

Wooden beads are carved in the same way as bone beads. Wood with a pronounced grain is usually turned in simple shapes, spheres or ovals to display it to advantage. Good quality, hard wood with a dense grain is used for carving or inlaid work. The inlaid work is achieved by carving the bead with a shape and then inserting a sliver of contrast colour wood or other materials cut in the same shape. Painted wooden beads are made from soft wood and varnished or stained with bright or subtle colours. They may also be highly decorated with abstract or pictorial designs or made into colourful animal, fish and fruit shapes. Lacquer (a substance made from the sap of the sumac tree) is used as a finish on wooden beads. The lacquer used to make Chinese carved cinnabar beads is stained with cinnabar (a vermilion-coloured pigment). The bead is brushed with as many as sixty coats of lacquer – each coat must dry thoroughly before the next and takes about half a day. This process from start to finish takes more than thirty days! Finally the bead is carved with the design.

Amber

Amber, a fossilized pine tree resin around fifty million years old, was one of the earliest highly prized bead materials. The most common colours are honey tones (often with small pieces of organic matter trapped inside) and shades of opaque yellow. The Baltic coastline has yielded the richest deposits. It is a costly material – the best quality is shaped into polished beads or cabochons, the less expensive into rough chips or nuggets.

Pearl

Pearls are naturally formed in nacre-producing shell fish who surround a small irritant inside its shell with layers of nacreous secretion. The most expensive pearls are large, well-formed, and highly lustrous. Tiny, round pearls are known as 'seed' pearls, mis-shapen ones as 'baroque'. Pearls may be successfully cultivated by artificially inserting a piece of grit into the shell of the mollusc which then coats it in nacre. Most 'cultured' pearls are very costly. More modestly priced are small, rice shaped,

freshwater pearls produced by the Japanese. These are formed by a number of tiny pieces of grit inserted into the shell, the knobbliest having as many as 40 inclusions!

Ivory

Ivory, procured from animal tusks has always been an expensive material because of its scarcity and the dangers involved in obtaining it. The nature of the material is both dense and tough so the most intricate and delicate designs can be carved. This makes it a perfect gem material and fine pieces could command a very high price but the trade is a cruel one and now illegal. The Chinese and Indians produce large quantities of remarkably finely carved beads of bone which have often been stained or smoked to look like old ivory.

Coral

Coral is formed from the calcified secretions of certain sea creatures which they build into the complex plant-like structures they inhabit. It may be carved quite intricately, made into beads or smooth cabochons. Though the majority of coral used for jewellery is a deep, pinky-red colour, it ranges from pale pink to white or black. Coral has been so extensively over-harvested that supplies are increasingly rare and quantities are controlled because coral takes many years to grow.

Jet

Jet is a shiny black, fossilized wood which, when cut and polished, has a high gloss. Carved jet jewellery and buttons have been found in Yorkshire dating from as early as 18000 BC; Whitby is one of the chief sources of the world's supply. Jet became very popular in England in the Victorian era, when it was worn as mourning jewellery, carved and faceted for brooches, beads and pendants and made into tiny cut beads and bugles for embroidering dresses. Amber, pearls, ivory, coral and jet are sometimes as highly valued as semi-precious or precious stones.

Above Semi-precious organic materials: a long string of faceted jet beads and a string of carved Whitby jet (courtesy of Stefany Tomalin, Beads, Portobello Road), a string of round pink coral beads, red coral chips, strings of small, naturally coloured freshwater pearls and a string of fine quality large oval Biwa freshwater pearls from Japan

Precious and semi-precious stones

Precious or semi-precious materials are prized for their intrinsic beauty and their ability to be fashioned into gems; scarcity usually determining their value. The most costly stones – diamonds, rubies, sapphires, emeralds and topaz are usually cut, polished and set in precious metal, whilst the more inexpensive are carved and drilled to make into beads. Even the waste chips from this process are smoothed and drilled for stringing.

Most transparent stones are of a crystalline nature, the colour often being affected by the materials that surround them. Certain stones may look different yet share the same crystal structure e.g. rubies and sapphire have the same nature as emerald and aquamarine. Transparent stones are often faceted to maximise their light-reflecting potential and intensity of colour to produce the richest and most brilliant effect. The hard, brittle nature of the material makes many precious stones difficult to drill and because they are sold by weight, it decreases the value.

Opaque, translucent stones or those with strange markings are smoothly rounded to display their particular characteristics like the inner glow of cat's eye, the blue shimmer of moonstone and the fiery depths of opal. Agates are often cut in this way to show their bands of colour and lacy, tree-like patterns.

The tougher gem stones lend themselves to the most beautiful and intricate carving. Jade, whether it is the costly 'Imperial' type or the more common nephrite can only be carved with a diamond-tipped tool. Other tougher stones are carnelian and turquoise.

From very early times it was believed widely that these precious materials were of heavenly origin and that a special relationship existed between certain stones and certain planets, which caused their particular powers to be enhanced during the phases of the planetary influences. Certain stones became associated with Zodiac signs, and later with the months of the year.

A number of less expensive stones began to be substituted or considered alternatives for the costly, precious gems so that the fashion of wearing birthstones (originally by the wealthy) has become more and more popular. See opposite for the current list of stones of the month published by the National Association of Goldsmiths of Great Britain.

Nowadays, in the West at least, the more extravagant claims about the mystic power of stones are dismissed as superstition. However, there still lingers a faint belief in 'good luck' charms and some stones, particularly crystals, are considered to have healing qualities.

January	**Garnet**	deep burgundy red, purplish red
February	**Amethyst**	transparent purple
March	**Aquamarine**	transparent sky or sea blue
	Bloodstone	green flecked with red
April	**Diamond**	clear with fiery flashes
	Rock crystal	clear
May	**Emerald**	deep transparent green
	Chrysoprase	opaque apple green
June	**Pearl**	
	Moonstone	white with blue shimmer
July	**Ruby**	rich, blood-red
	Carnelian	orangey-red
	Onyx	white with markings
August	**Peridot**	golden-green
	Sardonyx	red and white bands
September	**Sapphire**	transparent blue/pink/yellow
	Lapis lazuli	dark blue, gold veins
October	**Opal**	cloudy, with fiery inside glow
	Tourmaline	transparent pink and green
November	**Topaz**	golden to amber
	Citrine	transparent yellow to golden
December	**Turquoise**	opaque, blue-green

Above Assorted semi-precious stone beads and pendants including carved rose quartz, lapis, carnelian, serpentine (pale green), rock crystal, bowenite (brownish), moss agate (dark green) and amethyst. 'Donuts' of tiger's eye and turquoise and an arrow head of 'leopard' jasper

chapter two

Clay, Ceramic and Lac Beads

Clay is a universal, naturally occurring substance – earth and moisture combining to form a plastic mass which can be moulded into various shapes. The colour is determined by the mineral and vegetable matter which produce shades of yellow, ochre, pinky reds, rich brown, bluish greys and blacks.

Clay

Clay was one of the first materials manipulated by man to create amulets, beads, and other body ornaments. The earliest beads were simply rolled between the fingers, easily pierced, marked with patterns using sharp twigs or pieces of stone and then left to dry naturally in the sun. It was later discovered that baking the beads in a kiln made the shapes more durable, changing the colour of the clay according to the degree of heat applied. Terra-cotta – literally 'cooked earth', a brick red colour is achieved in this way. Clay beads would be decorated with coloured pigments but it was with the discovery of glazes that the most permanent, non-porous ceramics were born.

Ceramic

The word 'ceramic' comes from the Greek 'keramos' meaning pottery ie. clay-based products coated with a vitreous glaze, baked in a kiln at high temperatures. This process makes the object more durable and produces beautiful, permanent colours.

A very early type of ceramic known to the ancient Egyptians was a material somewhere between ceramic and glass, made of pulverized quartz and clay. This clay compound had amounts of glass-making constituents which, when baked at high temperatures, produced a glassy crust on the surface. The most common colour was turquoise influenced by the minerals in the soil – iron creates a more greenish tone and copper creates a more bluish tone – although yellows, ochres and pinks were also possible. This material is known as 'Egyptian paste' or more commonly 'Egyptian faience' though the latter term is the name of a type of glaze. Round- and tube-shaped beads spaced with gold were used in earrings, bracelets and necklaces, particularly the traditional multi-stranded collars worn by Egyptians. The material was frequently cast in the form of amulets or charms in the images of various gods. Most famous of these is the turquoise scarab (the dung beetle) which is the symbol of the god of the heavens rolling the sun across the sky. Beads inscribed with magical inscriptions were worn to protect against the evil eye. Even nowadays, as well as creating beads in various colours, Egyptian bead designers still make copies of the original shapes in the traditional turquoise blue.

Above Necklace of ancient Egyptian faience beads from Charlotte Smith's collection

Left Modern copies of traditional Egyptian faience shapes, Peruvian terracotta beads marked with traditional geometric patterns and large oval white-patterned terracotta bead from Africa

Methods of making clay and ceramic beads

Clay beads are often made using the traditional methods but most are baked in a kiln for durability. They may be coated with glazes containing various metallic pigments and fired to produce bright, vitreous colours. The rarest type of feldspar clay is kaolin, named after the region Kao Ling, in which it was first discovered by the Chinese in 3000 BC. Kaolin (also known as china clay) is used to make the delicate yet tough white ceramic – porcelain. Its white surface provides a perfect base for decoration.

Hand-moulded clay and ceramic beads are usually solid, rolled between the fingers and pierced with metal wire or rods whilst the clay is still in a plastic state, then dried or fired in a kiln on rods. They vary in shape from the fine, delicately hand-decorated beads made by the Peruvians, to the more robust and primitive beads in the bold, colourful glazes favoured by the Africans and the Greeks.

Peruvian beads

The Peruvian beads we see today originated in the late 1970s when the painters of Peruvian ceramics used scaled down versions of their traditional Inca forms – miniature llamas, birds and suns – to decorate delicate beads of different shapes. The original tiny beads were all hand-moulded – the round ones rolled between the palms of the hands and the tube shapes made from coils of clay rolled into a long cylinder which would be cut, pierced, allowed to dry naturally, then fired, painted and individually lacquered. Many round beads are still made in this way, but the cylinder shapes are now mostly made using an apparatus based on the old mincing machine, which saves a lot of time and has greatly increased output. A further development has been the use of imported porcelain clay which can be fired to high temperatures to preserve the definition of the detailed motifs in strong enamelled colours.

Porcelain beads

Porcelain beads made with white kaolin clay are often hollow and cast in moulds. The fineness of the clay ensures a smooth, even finish, well suited to the type of delicate enamelling traditional to Chinese beadmakers. Porcelain can be fired to very high temperatures to produce a hard, durable yet slightly translucent material which absorbs glazes beautifully. To make these hollow beads, the clay is mixed with sufficient water to make a creamy consistency. The liquid clay (known as 'slip') is trickled into plaster moulds which are then spun at high speed to coat the inside with an evenly distributed layer. Because the plaster mould is very porous, it quickly sucks the moisture from the slip, leaving a thin shell of clay. Once sufficiently dry, the beads are released from the moulds – any cutting and piercing is done at this stage, then the porcelain is fired in a kiln. The matt finish produced after this firing is called 'bisque' or 'biscuit'. Then the beads are decorated as a small degree of porosity remains in the surface, to which the colours adhere very well. If the bead has been

glazed before decorating, the colours applied remain raised on the surface and can be seen and felt.

Whether the bead is entirely coated with colour or whether a design is painted on, the only permanent colours are enamels made from metallic oxide pigments fused to the surface by firing in a kiln. As different enamel colours change or attain their intensity at different temperatures, a bead decorated with many colours may need multiple firings at successively lower temperatures.

The strongest colourant of all is cobalt, which produces various shades of blue, probably one of the earliest colours used for decoration; this is the pigment used in the traditional blue and white Chinese porcelain beads. Violet, cream, brown and black shades are obtained from manganese; uranium will produce yellows, oranges and reds; chrome gives greens, reds and browns and tin produces a white glaze as well as making other colours opaque. The richest and most costly reds and purples are achieved by the addition of gold.

Decoration is applied to the surface by painting with a mixture of liquid pigments and a certain amount of gum to help the colours adhere. It is fired, sometimes several times for beads with many colours, then coated with a clear glaze. The beads may also be enamelled after glazing, and highlighted with lines of gilding. Sometimes the surface decoration is applied by transfer; these transfers which are usually floral, are called 'decals'.

A lustred finish may be obtained by the addition of carbon to the other minerals – copper carbonate produces red, salmon or golden lustres; silver carbonate yellowish or ivory lustres, whilst bismuth is used to produce an iridescent coating.

Above right Richly glazed, solid ceramic beads from Africa. The rings and lustred pink bead are Greek

Above left Decorated porcelain beads which include: Chinese cloisonné style or traditional cobalt blue and white, American cylindrical porcelain beads, striped to resemble glass chevron beads and solid beads from Rajasthan, hand-decorated with the traditional floral motifs used in their pottery

Above 'Feathering' a striped lac cane; the technique is also known as 'combing'

Lac beads

Lac beads are really a category of their own, being neither clay nor plastic, but are moulded into shape in a similar way. They are made from a substance produced by a prolific Oriental insect, the lac beetle (the name comes from the Hindi word 'lakh', meaning 100,000). The creature lives by ingesting the resin of the tree and exudes a sticky substance which it deposits on the branches. This resinous substance is collected, boiled down and formed into little flat cakes. The material is expensive as it takes very many beetles a long time to produce very little; the clearer the colour – a reddish amber – the more costly it is. For the purpose of beadmaking the lac is reheated to melt it down and mixed with a plasticizing filler to form a clay-like substance which is malleable when hot, but cools to a durable hardness. This greyish lac 'clay' is often used to form a supporting base for silver or white metal beads, amulets and pendants. It is moulded into the required shape, then wrapped with thin sheet metal and inscribed or enamelled. The lac can also be stained with bright colours to decorate the grey base. It is sometimes studded with tiny stones or pieces of coloured glass mirror.

Indian coloured lac beads are made somewhat in the manner of glass beads, that is from 'canes' or rods of the raw material. Dyed lac is shaped into tablets of brilliant colour stuck on wooden sticks – these are used to decorate the bead cane. A ball of grey lac 'clay' is moulded onto the end of a stick, heated over a charcoal burner and then rolled into a cylindrical shape over a stone marvering (smoothing) block. The beadmaker then takes a tablet of coloured lac which he holds over the hot charcoal until the surface melts sufficiently to coat the cane; he may use a single colour if he wants to make mono-coloured beads, but more frequently the dyed lac is applied in stripes or random patches of two or more colours. He rolls the lac cylinder over the stone block, using a small wooden marvering tool to assist in elongating and reducing it until it becomes a long cane of the required thickness.

This is then cut from the main cylinder and left to cool and harden; it will later be reheated before being used to shape into beads. The beadmaker can produce a candy-striped cane by twisting it as he rolls it out so that the stripes of colour spiral around the surface. Alternatively, a marbled or 'feathered' effect can be achieved by dragging a pointed tool backwards and forwards across the stripes before rolling out and reducing the cane.

Other more random decoration may be achieved by using 'threads' of colour pulled out from a softened, dyed lac tablet or 'crumbs' of crumbled lac. A glittery cane may be formed by suspending golden flecks in the resin. This latter is expensive, not least because the best quality, clearest lac must be used.

To make the beads, a cane of the appropriate thickness is softened over the charcoal burner and a section of the correct length (judged by eye) is cut with a large pair of scissors. This is then quickly moulded into a rough shape with the fingers and finished off in a pre-cast mould or by rolling over a smooth, heat-proof glass plate. The bead is pierced with an awl whilst still hot and then left to cool and harden. When trying out a new shape, a mould is made initially from lac; once the beadmaker is satisfied with the shape, a brass mould is made, which produces a sharper outline.

Below Assorted bead shapes made from lac canes

Indian lac beads are made by a small team of three or four people, often a family group. The entire process, from start to finish is painstaking and time consuming; it can take a full day to produce between 400-500 beads.

chapter three

Metal Beads

The earliest metal beads were made from gold, silver and copper. During the Bronze and Iron Ages in Sumeria, Assyria and Egypt, these metals were cast, drawn into wire, worked into granulated beads, beaten into sheets and soldered to make hollow beads. The use of gold in jewellery was so common in ancient Egypt that the hieroglyph for gold was the drawing of a collar of beads.

In subsequent centuries all over the world, metal beads have formed an integral part of bead jewellery making. The Greeks and Romans used a great deal of gold in their jewellery – the beads were often highly decorated with filigree wire or tiny granules of gold to make the most lavish adornment. Plain beads were made from beaten sheets of metal that was so fine it was almost paper thin. They were generally used with semi-precious beads and stones.

Above and below African hammered pendants of aluminium and brass

Far right Strings of African aluminium beads (the light-coloured metal) and steel beads

Metal bead materials

Gold has always been a costly metal and its use in bead production has become increasingly rare. Today it features mostly as small, hollow round and tubular spacers between larger beads made from other materials. Silver is still widely used and many fine beads are made using ancient techniques. However, the bulk of current bead production is from metal alloys (a mixture of two or more metals), notably brass (golden) from copper and zinc and white metal or German silver, from copper, zinc and nickel.

Even gold and silver need to be alloyed with small amounts of other metals to make them hard enough for working. The proportions are usually regulated by law – silver (alloyed with copper) must be a minimum 92.5% before it is allowed to be called Sterling. However standards vary from one country to another and in India good quality silver beads are generally about 80%. Gold is alloyed with copper, silver, palladium and nickel. The purest gold is 24 carat (referring to the amount of gold in the alloy), the highest amount generally used is 22 carat (91.6%) and the lowest is 9 carat (37.5%). The term 'carat' originates from the Arabic word for the carob bean, which was used as a measure of weight for pearls by Oriental traders.

A way of achieving the appearance of gold and silver is to plate a base metal with a layer of the precious metal. This is generally done by electrolysis. The object is immersed in an acid bath together with a piece of the plating metal. An electric current is passed through the bath, which causes a certain amount of the precious metal to be attracted to the base metal, thus forming a coating around the object. The thickness of this layer depends on the length of the process and the strength of the current passed through the acid.

The gold surface on rolled gold and gold filled metal is obtained by fusing together a sandwich of copper between two sheets of gold and rolling it out to the desired thickness. In the case of rolled gold, the surface layers may be fairly thin and therefore are not as durable as the superior gold filled metal where the gold content has to be of at least 10 carat quality and not less than 1/20th of the total weight.

Silver tarnishes naturally with age and even more rapidly if kept in damp conditions. To keep it looking shiny, it can be polished from time to time either with a soft cloth (wool is particularly good) or with silver polish (though this tends to leave a greyish deposit in hollows and grooves and is not recommended for filigree beads). An antique patina often adds to the attraction of silver – many modern silver or silver-plated beads are given an appearance of age by immersing them in a solution of potassium polysulphide. The longer the metal is left in the solution the darker the colour will become.

Aluminium is occasionally used for beadmaking. In Africa, recycled drinks cans are reworked to make rough beads and flat hammered pendants inscribed with animal or other shapes.

Iron alone is rarely used now for jewellery because it rusts. Steel, which is iron hardened with carbon, and made stainless by the addition of chromium is occasionally used for beads by African beadmakers.

Methods of metal beadmaking

Although the bulk of modern bead production is from non-precious materials, the ancient metal working techniques still survive, in spite of increased mechanization for mass production, and much metal beadmaking employs a degree of hand work.

Metal beads are made from solid, mould-cast shapes or are hollow, stamped out of sheet metal. The former are generally made in pre-shaped, two-part moulds, usually metal, but occasionally clay – the molten metal is poured into the closed mould and when cooled is released. Smaller beads are mass-produced in multiple moulds. An ancient method of casting, the 'lost wax technique' is still in use today particularly in Africa to make metal figurines, animal shapes and head pendants. First the object is modelled in wax, then coated in clay with a small opening. Once the clay is dry, the mould is heated until the wax melts and is 'lost' through the opening. Molten metal is poured into this and allowed to cool. The mould is then broken to reveal the object. This technique allows only a single piece to be made which can never be exactly duplicated.

Hollow beads are made from sheet metal – silver, brass and occasionally copper – stamped with half the bead shape, cut, then the halves soldered together. Small hollow beads can be made from metal tubing. The metal can be smooth or shaped

Below American cast metal beads and pendants with 'antique' finish, the brass turtle (top left) is African, made by the 'lost wax' technique (these shapes were used as weights for gold)

while it is being drawn, to form a fluted surface. Tubing of the required diameter is cut into sections which are placed in a punching machine fitted with a die of the shape to be made – cylindrical, oval, conical, round or teardrop.

If the sheet metal is beaten very fine, it needs to be supported so that it does not collapse inwards when the bead is worked. The bead shape is moulded in a solid material like lac or resin and then the thin metal is wrapped around it.

The inscribing of designs on sheet metal is known as 'chasing' and is a very ancient technique. The pattern is made by hammering a chisel into the surface of the metal so that the design is impressed into it. Repoussé work is the reverse of this – the design is hammered from the back so that it appears raised on the surface.

Decorations

Other types of metal work commonly used as decoration in beadmaking are filigree work, granulation, and enamelling or cloisonné work. The two former were techniques known during the Bronze age, widely adopted by the ancient Greeks and Etruscans, who were superb metal workers, and have been practised ever since. Enamelling and cloisonné work are also ancient forms of metal decoration – the earliest known uses of these were in Egypt in about 1600 BC. Fine examples of this work were widespread in Byzantium in 6 AD. In the sixteenth and seventeenth centuries, enamelling played a very important part in jewellery making throughout Europe.

Filigree is made from wire soldered together to form a pattern; this pattern may be open work or the wire may be soldered onto a solid base in coils, loops or scrolls.

Granulation is a type of decoration whereby tiny round 'grains' of silver or gold are soldered onto the base. The grains are formed in the following way – tiny pieces or filings of gold or silver are sprinkled onto powdered charcoal and heated in a metal container. As the scraps of metal melt, they form themselves into little balls.

Above left Indian and Chinese hollow metal beads, Spanish stampings – flat pendants embossed and stamped out of thin sheet metal, coiled wire beads and Chinese and Turkish filigree beads

Above right Indian and Balinese hollow silver beads with embossing, granulation and coiled wire decoration (those with the heaviest oxidation and more elaborate granulation are from Bali), Thai silver and white metal beads moulded around a resin base and small Turkish granulated beads

Right Chinese cloisonné beads – in some cases not all of the 'cloisons' have been filled with enamel but have been gilded or silver plated instead. The red beads with cloisonné band are cinnabar lacquered and carved

Left Chinese enamelled beads and bead caps – some beads have cut metal designs of dragons and flowers, Chinese articulated enamelled fish pendants, Nepalese brass based beads set with roundels of red and turquoise glass and yellow, blue and green Moroccan beads with silver granulation

Once cool, they are sorted into sizes by being shaken in a series of sieves. The bead is coated with an adhesive paste and the grains of metal are placed on it one by one to form a pattern, then soldered to fix them in position.

Enamelling on beads is the process of applying colour by firing a paste made from powdered glass onto the surface of the metal. This method produces brilliant transparent colours enhanced by the metal shining through from below, or delicate pastels when opaque enamel is used. After the firing, the exposed metal is polished, or if a copper base is used, gold or silver plated.

The colours on cloisonné-enamelled beads go through a number of processes to bake the enamel hard on the surface of the metal. The body of the bead is made from two half-spheres of copper soldered together. Copper wire, coiled in the required design, is soldered onto the body. The little compartments thus formed are known as 'cloisons', from the French word meaning 'cells'; hence the name of the process. The enamelling powder is applied and fired in at least three stages until the colour entirely fills the cloisons. The bead then goes through two separate polishings, the first to remove any roughness and irregularities on the surface of the bead and the second to bring it up to its finished gloss. Finally the exposed copper wire is gilded or silver-plated. The stages involved in the making of a cloisonné bead are shown below:

 Bodymaking

 Wiring, soldering

 Colouring, firing (first)

 Colouring, firing (second)

 Colouring, firing (final)

 Polishing

 Polishing (final)

 Gilding

chapter four

Glass Beads

Glass is the most versatile material for making beads. In its heated softened state, glass can be manipulated into an infinite variety of shapes – blown into feather-light bubbles, moulded into solid spheres of colour and pulled into hair-fine strands. In its cooled state, it becomes hard and glossy and can be cut, ground and polished in the same way as precious stones. Because of these qualities and its extraordinary range of colours, glass has been used to imitate precious and semi-precious stones very successfully since ancient times.

In 15000 BC glass beads appeared in abundance throughout Egypt and Mesopotamia. Glass was very highly valued in its own right, often being set in gold or strung with gold beads. It followed the manufacture of faience, a type of glazed ceramic widely used in Egyptian jewellery, which shared the same basic constituents. By 12000 BC the Phoenicians were making elaborate glass beads in a number of colours, many with stylized depictions of 'eyes' – these were considered efficacious as a charm against the evil eye. The Phoenician craftsmen were also responsible for devising the technique of 'mosaic' work using complex canes of glass with geometric shapes which became widespread throughout the Mediterranean and subsequently throughout Europe by the time of the Roman Empire. Other early techniques used in beadmaking were hollow blown glass and 'gold-in-glass', in which a layer of gold foil was sandwiched between the core of the bead and the surface transparent layer.

During the Middle Ages very little jewellery was worn and glass beads fell out of favour. There was no large scale production of glass beads for jewellery until the fifteenth century when the ancient beadmaking techniques were revived in Europe by the Venetians, major international traders, whose glass making skills were foremost in the world.

Below The most famous of African trade beads are those with mosaic or millefiori decoration. From the sixteenth century, the Venetians manufactured and traded mosaic beads, though most now found in Africa were exported from Venice around the latter half of the nineteenth century

The greatest expansion and distribution of glass beads took place during the nineteenth century with the enormous increase in trade between the nations of the world. Although the principal manufacturers of glass beads were the Venetians, by this time their secrets had travelled to Holland and Gablonsk, Bohemia where there were a number of thriving industries producing fine quality glass beads. Sparkling and richly coloured beads were instantly appealing to people whose culture placed a very high value on body ornamentation and the wealthy European nations soon capitalized on this. Glass beads were made by the ton and then shipped around the world and traded for furs, gold, ivory and other rare commodities.

The basic techniques of glass beadmaking are now fairly widely known and practised in similar ways by most beadmakers. However, each major manufacturer has a particular speciality or skill which is still jealously guarded. The Venetians remain producers of fine quality glass and masters of intricate mosaic work; they export glass canes and slices of mosaic glass cane called 'murrine' used to decorate beads. The Czechs and Austrians are renowned for the clarity and precision of their faceted crystal glass. The Japanese, too, are major manufacturers of excellent quality glass beads both fancy and plain, though these, like Venetian and Czech beads, are expensive. The most recent reasonably large scale production of fine quality handmade beads is in India, a country with a love of decoration and an ancient tradition of beadmaking, where techniques have greatly improved in recent years.

Above Glass beads from the African trade: these beads are European in origin, traded with Africa over the centuries, and now much sought after in the West. Graduated string of opaque red moulded oval beads, believed to have originated in Holland, a string of small red oval 'white hearts', so called as the core of the bead is of milk-white glass coated with a layer of transparent red, a string of opaque red discs from Ethiopia (believed to be Dutch) and a string of moulded glass snake beads from Bohemia dating c. 1920s

Above Two Indian glass workers stretch a softened cylinder of glass into a long thin cane using heated iron rods, to which the glass adheres. Glass beads are made from these coloured canes

Right Strings of African Trade beads of European origin: turquoise blue cylindrical beads, a string of round, dark blue hand-wound beads (believed to be Dutch), blue glass rings, tiny turquoise 'white heart' cylinders, yellow 'Vaseline' glass beads with moulded facets and a string of multi-coloured, transparent beads (both of Bohemian origin c. 1930s)

Constituents of glass beads

The main constituents of glass are silica (sand quartz), lime and soda or potash. When fired to a high temperature, these fuse together and become transparent, usually with a greenish tinge. Different colours are obtained by adding certain minerals to the basic ingredients – iron produces greens and blues and cobalt produces the deepest blues. There is no true black in glass, what appears to be black is usually a very dark purple which comes from manganese. The rarest and most expensive colours to make are the deep reds and pinks produced from the addition of gold. Lead is used both to brighten and intensify all colours and also to clarify transparent glass to a crystalline quality, hence the name of crystal. The colours are made opaque by adding calcium or tin. Opalescent shades with a filmy, milky quality are achieved either by the addition of bone ash or by controlling the melting process so that some of the crystals remain unmelted. 'Goldstone' or aventurine glass is a transparent glass with tiny specks of copper which give it a sparkling appearance. The most common colour is golden, though there is a blue glass version as well. This glass is most frequently used for decoration of the bead.

Methods of glass beadmaking

The best quality glass must be heated and cooled several times to clarify it and to eliminate any air bubbles which can cause flaws and cracking. Because of the number of variables, it is very difficult to achieve absolute consistency from one batch to another. After the glass ingredients are heated and melted, the lower quality glass is made into 'cakes' for reheating in a furnace; these are used to make the cheaper glass beads. The superior quality is drawn into rods of various thicknesses ('canes') and are reserved for lamp work. The rods or canes of coloured glass are made by stretching out a cylindrical mass of softened glass into long lengths. The four chief types of glass bead in production today are hand-wound, drawn hollow cane, hollow blown and moulded.

Hand-wound beads

This method produces beads ranging from the plainest coloured glass with little or no decoration, to the finest, most intricately detailed work. The simplest hand-wound beads are those made directly from the molten glass in the furnace. This method generally produces rather coarse, large beads with large holes blackened from the iron rods on which they are made. The finest hand-wound beads are 'lamp beads', so-called because they are made from glass canes worked over a lamp flame. These beads are made individually by winding the softened end of a glass cane onto a wire, then rolling it in a mould to perfect the shape. Any subsequent decoration is made by reheating the bead over the flame and 'painting' it with fine filaments of glass.

Above left Furnace and lamp wound beads with spot, eye and 'crumb' decoration. The beads with raised concentric rings of colour are copies of old eye beads made by the English bead maker, Bill Tufnell. The large gilded eye bead is called 'Polifemo' by the Venetian beadmakers, after the mythological one-eyed giant and the matt blue ovals are Indonesian 'eye' beads

The simplest form of decoration is achieved by using fine, single coloured canes. These are used to apply dots or trails of contrast colour to the surface of the bead; stripes and spirals are achieved by melting a trail of glass onto the surface of the bead which is turned steadily in the lamp flame. The glass can also be applied to form wavy lines or zig-zags. 'Scrabble' decoration is achieved by one or more colours being dotted in an entirely random manner. All of these patterns may be left raised on the surface of the bead or marvered smooth. A 'feathered' effect is achieved by dragging a pointed metal tool across stripes or rings of glass on the surface while the bead is still malleable. Beads with a spot or circle of different colour on the main body of the bead have come to be termed 'eye' beads. Since the earliest times in numerous cultures the coloured spot has been considered symbolic of the human eye and was thought to give the wearer protection against the evil eye. The more elaborate the arrangement of spots or the more 'eye-like', the more powerful the magic was held to be.

A twisted glass cane used particlarly in Venetian beads is the 'lace cane' also known as 'filigrano' (filigree). This is made from clear glass canes combined with coloured ones; the favourite colour, an opaque milky white, known as 'lattecino', is made by twisting white and clear canes together and then encasing them with a layer of clear glass. This complex cane is drawn out so the pattern becomes finer and produces a lacy effect.

One of the most beautiful hand-wound beads is the Venetian 'fiorato' (flowered) bead, in which fine glass canes are used to produce flower shapes – roses and

leaves, sometimes gilded or decorated with goldstone scrolls. The decoration is often left raised on the surface or only lightly marvered (smoothed) in.

A characteristic type of Czech lamp bead is one in which the glass core, often of opalescent glass, is decorated with swirls of colour or floral shapes and then coated with a layer of transparent glass.

The Roman 'gold-in-glass' bead was the forerunner of the foiled glass bead developed by the Venetians, the Czechs and now the Japanese. Modern versions often have floral patterns, abstract splashes or swirls of colour superimposed over a middle layer of silver foil which are then coated with clear or coloured transparent glass. The foil both intensifies the colour and imparts an extra depth of lustre to the bead. A yellow- or amber-coloured coat over silver foil gives the appearance of gold. Goldstone (aventurine) glass is often used in a similar way to give an inner sparkle to transparent, coloured glass.

Very early in the history of glass working a complex, multi-coloured cane was devised to produce a mosaic or 'millefiori' (thousand flower) bead. Abstract, floral or even pictorial patterns can be produced by arranging a number of canes of different colours together to form a pattern. Once the glass has cooled, slices known as 'murrine' (little tiles) are cut from it. These are used to decorate a base bead. The beadmaker positions them on the bead, which he reheats in the lamp flame, so that they fuse together, and then marvers it smooth in the mould. The entire surface may be covered with the mosaics laid side by side. The Venetians are the most skilled practitioners of this type of work; famous for their multi-coloured star and flower patterns.

Above Decorating a bead with spots of glass from a twisted glass cane

Top left An assortment of Indian, Czechoslovakian and Venetian finely worked lamp beads, some with surface gilding, goldstone, gold or silver foil core; some with fiorata, filigree or lace cane decoration. Most of these beads are in current production

Top right Mosaic and millefiori beads: some are old Venetian ones from the African Trade (cylindrical, matt opaque colours). The large, round bead (centre) with chevron decoration is a modern Venetian bead and the others are Indian in current production

Drawn hollow cane beads

The beads so far described have been made using solid glass canes; the wire on which they have been wound forming the perforation. The hollow-drawn cane bead incorporates the perforation in its manufacture, allowing a speedier production. Though nowadays production is increasingly mechanized, particularly in the manufacture of small beads for embroidery or weaving, the traditional methods are still in use for the making of larger, fancy beads. The process is the same as that described for solid cane making, except that a hollow pipe is used to collect the gather of glass instead of a solid iron rod. The beadmaker blows down the pipe to form a bubble of air in the glass gather. The hot glass is then drawn out and the bubble inside it is elongated to form a long tube with the hole running throughout its length. When the tube has decreased to the required thickness it is laid to cool and then cut into sections. The rough edges may be hand ground or smoothed by tumbling in sand.

The coloured lining inside transparent beads is applied after the manufacture of the hollow cane by sucking liquid silver, gold or coloured pigment into the tube either mechanically or by mouth. Amber glass with a silver lining appears golden.

Above Indian beadmaker blowing a bubble of air into a chevron cane; as the glass is drawn out, the bubble will form a hole throughout its length

Below Beads made from slices and sections of cylindrical, triangular or squared drawn hollow cane – the long thin tubes, usually used for bead curtains, are Indian, the others are made in the USA

The most dramatic of all drawn hollow cane beads is the 'chevron' (also known as the 'paternoster', 'rosetta' or 'star' bead) which is believed to have been invented by the Venetians in the fifteenth century. The chevron became one of the most highly prized beads of the African trade and is still treasured today. The bead has several layers of different colours and is usually cylindrical in shape, the ends displaying the characteristic star or chevron pattern around a central core. Although other colours exist, it generally has a white hollow cane core with alternating layers of blue, white and red, finishing with a final layer of blue. The chevron cane is made in the same way as the mosaic canes already described – it may be moulded in star-shaped, tapered moulds or by assembling a number of coloured canes or strips of glass around the hollow core.

The drawn cane method most in use today is for the mass production of small single colour beads. The hollow cane is pulled out until it reduces to a fine tube; short sections of this tube are cut, put into a large metal drum together with very fine sand and ash and tumbled over heat to polish and smooth the edges. The sand and ash fill the holes in the tube sections so that the glass does not distort and collapse inwards in the heat. The longer the beads are tumbled, the rounder they become. The beads are then sorted into size by shaking them in a series of sieves with different grades of mesh from fine to large hole, so first of all the sand falls through, then the smallest beads, then the slightly larger and so on until they are all accurately graded.

Below String of old Venetian chevrons from Nancy Wall's collection; loose beads – the single, large barrel shape in traditional colours is Venetian, the others are Indian – some of these have only five or six points to the star shape

The manufacture of the tiniest of drawn cane beads is now highly mechanized. These beads are used in embroidery and bead weaving or as spacers between larger beads. They come in an extraordinarily wide range of colours from the basic transparent, translucent, opalescent and opaque colours to those with surface finish – iridescent, pearly or metallic lustres with silver, gold, or colour linings. They have a number of different names, the smallest often called 'seed' beads (because of their resemblance to plant seeds), 'love' beads (possibly because articles made from them were given as love tokens), and 'rocailles' after the French word meaning 'little rocks'. Bugle beads are small sections cut from fine tubes – these are given only a brief tumbling to smooth the sharp edges.

Right Rocailles ('seed' beads) and bugles are used for weaving, embroidery and as spacer beads. Shown here are opaque, transparent silver-lined, ceylon (pearly), rainbow, frosted and metallic coated beads

Hollow blown beads

Fragile, bubble beads of thin glass are formed from fine hollow tubes. The glass is heated, the hole stopped at the end, and the beadmaker blows a bubble of air into the tube. When cool, this bubble is broken off as a single bead. The rough edges around the holes are smoothed by gentle reheating. Multiple beads may be formed by pulling out the glass and elongating the bubble (the air trapped inside the glass ensures that it does not collapse inwards) – the resultant tube is then pinched at intervals to form beads using pincers or moulding tongs. Surface decoration may be applied to the glass tube, often stripes of coloured glass laid along its length.

Left Hollow glass beads: Chinese fish bead, two white lace cane beads made by Bill Tufnell and the others are Venetian. The decoration on the Venetian gold flecked beads is achieved by applying gold leaf to the hot glass before the bubble is blown. As the air expands the glass, it fractures the layer of gold leaf and produces the pattern that you see. The coloured spirals on the 'filigrano' beads are made by laying fine stripes of coloured cane along the hot glass tube and marvering these into the surface. As the bubble is blown, it is twisted so that the stripes spiral along its length, creating a delicate filigree effect. The designs on the Chinese beads are hand-painted on the interior, using hair-fine brushes

Moulded beads

Below West African powder glass beads. The small yellow biconical beads are known as 'chau-chau'. It can be seen clearly that the white and blue strung beads are made up of two halves which have been fused together

The earliest solid moulded beads were made in much the same way as the method currently adopted by African beadmakers. Powdered glass beads are fashioned of a paste made from crushed, recycled glass or from a type of glass mix which fuses together when heated but does not melt entirely – thus retaining a granular texture ('sand' beads). These beads are baked in a kiln in clay moulds which are coated in a fine clay slip to facilitate the removal of the beads after firing: wetted, slip-coated plant stalks are then inserted into the hollows and the bead paste is pressed into the hollows around the stalks, often layered in bands of different colours. In the firing process, the stalks are burnt away, leaving the beads with holes ready pierced.

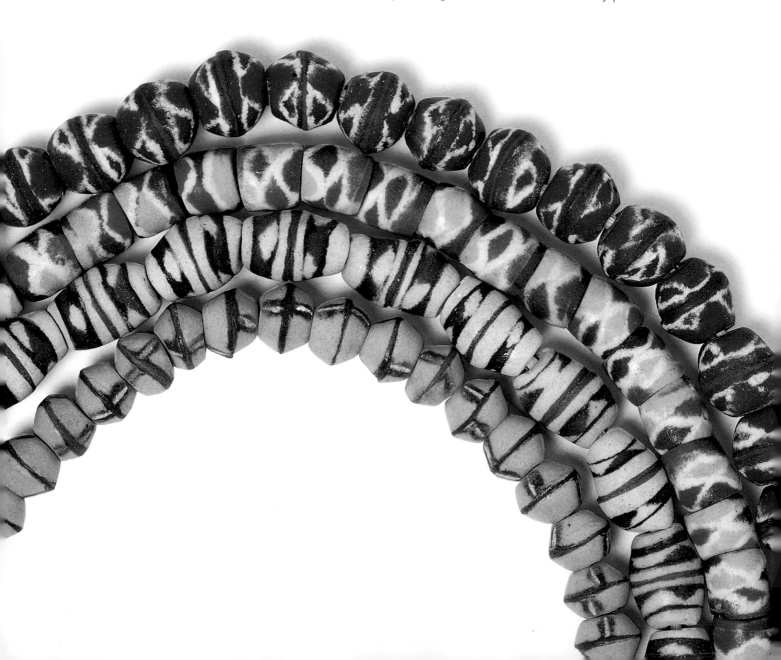

The base beads can then be decorated with trails of the powdered paste and refired. The favourite ground colour is yellow. 'Bodom' beads, highly prized in Ghana, are large round, yellow beads decorated with trails or 'eyes' in brown, blue or green. At one time they were valued as much as gold and only élite members of the social strata were allowed to wear them. 'Chau-chau' are biconical, decorated with stripes or eyes on a yellow or occasionally orange or green base and 'gashi' are cylindrical, built up with layers of different colours.

The colourful glass beads of Kiffa in Mauritania are usually bright scarlet or blue with fine yellow and black stripes or zig-zags and white-encircled blue 'eyes' (see title page). The decoration is accomplished by mixing coloured powdered glass with saliva or gum arabic and applying it painstakingly to the base bead with the use of a needle. The shapes may be spherical, barrel shaped, oval, conical or most characteristically, triangular, with the hole pierced across the apex; the latter shape being considered a powerful antidote to the evil eye.

Other early methods of bead moulding were done with hinged metal moulds mounted on tongs; these would be squeezed over the hot glass whilst it was still on the wire. When the bead was released, the excess glass squeezed through the mould would be ground away by hand. This mould produces only a single bead; next came a multiple mould which had prongs to pierce the beads as the two parts of the mould closed over the bead. In the simplest tong-operated moulds, the prong had to be slightly tapered so that it would be easily released from the cooling glass as the mould was opened. Beads made in this way show a slightly conical perforation with the hole larger at the point of entry of the prong.

Nowadays the more sophisticated and mechanized process is to use multiple moulds which are furnished with wires that pierce the softened glass beads. The moulds are mechanically lifted as they are opened so that the wire is withdrawn evenly with no distortion of the perforation. Thus, in a single operation a number of beads of uniform size and hole are formed. Apart from the usual bead shapes – spherical, oval, barrel etc. – this process allows quite complex shapes to be made like 'faceted' beads and fruit, flower and animal shapes.

Right Moulded glass beads: round machine-pressed beads, beads with machine pressed or cut facets and assorted shapes (all Czech). The green glass heart with wire loops is Indian and other shapes on wire are Japanese

Beads are often given a surface coating or lustre: iridescent or rainbow effects are achieved by vaporizing certain metals to produce a deposit on the surface of the beads. Pearls have been imitated in glass for as long as there has been the technology to simulate their nacreous lustre. In the nineteenth century, a French beadmaker invented a pearly coating made from pounded fish scales which was known as 'essence d'orient'. Hollow glass beads were coated on the inside with this substance and then filled with wax to give them the required weight. Later, the French perfected an opaline glass with a pearly lustre; hollow beads made from this were filled with a type of gum. Today the best simulated pearls are made with a surface or interior coating derived from 'essence d'orient'. Cheaper imitation glass pearls are dipped or sprayed with a pearly lacquer akin to nail polish whilst strung and evidence of this coating is usually visible.

Left Austrian and Czech cut or pressed beads with rainbow, lustred or iris coatings. Lustred lozenge and twisted shapes are Indian. Glass based pearl-coated beads from Czechoslovakia (smooth shapes) and Japan (baroque shapes)

chapter five

Plastic Beads

Below left Italian plastic beads with marbled and gold dusted finish

Below right Italian plastic imitating stone, 'antique' terracotta and other natural materials

The first plastics commercially available were made in the mid-nineteenth century from chemically treated organic compounds – wood fibre with nitric or acetic acids – which became known as cellulose, and caseinate (milk protein treated with formaldehyde). Apart from their industrial uses, they were widely used in jewellery. Celluloid and Galalith (from the Greek words meaning 'milk' and 'stone') were used both for beads and also to imitate a variety of precious materials like amber, tortoiseshell and ivory. However, they had disadvantages. Celluloid was highly inflammable and the caseinates, because they absorbed moisture, deteriorated quickly, becoming discoloured and pitted.

By the turn of the century, less flammable, more durable plastics were developed. Coal tar was used as a base, then treated with formaldehyde and other additives to give colour and weight. One of the most famous of these – 'Bakelite' – imitates very successfully the more opaque type of yellowish amber and is frequently mistaken for the real thing. These early plastics were opaque or semi-translucent, imitating such materials as amber, coral, jet, ivory, tortoiseshell, and mother-of-pearl. By the 1920s, petroleum-based compounds were used to develop much brighter acrylic plastics with clear, jewel-like colours. This led to the mass production of cheap, imitation gemstone jewellery which was despised by the purists for being garish and tawdry.

However, improved techniques of casting and moulding and more sophisticated surface finishes combined with the increasingly expensive raw material now place the plastic bead in high esteem. Cheap and gaudy fake 'gems' are still to be found but there is also a range of superior quality beads in subtle as well as bright colours, with surface frosting or iridescent sheen and cores of silver which impart a luminous depth. Metal plating methods have improved so that not only bright gold and silver finishes are available but also matt, 'antique' and verdigris patina.

The ease with which plastic can be moulded into clean lines or complex shapes means that it is possible to produce dramatic beads and interesting shapes for jewellery. See the modern, sophisticated Italian-made plastics, copies of ancient gold, silver, or copper Roman and Byzantine shapes, and those with the delicate effect of gold-dusted, blown Venetian glass.

Above left Italian plastic beads with antiqued metallic finishes

Above right Japanese beads with iridescent coatings: Japanese plastic 'miracle' beads with a layer of silver foil sandwiched between core and surface layer and Italian plastic in frosted transparent colours and coloured metallic finishes (the larger ones)

Methods of plastic beadmaking

There are three main methods of producing plastic beads – compression moulding, injection moulding and extrusion. The two former methods employ the same dies that are used for casting metal – beads may also be made from sections cut from extruded tubes of plastic. To make moulded plastic beads, plastic powder or chippings are poured into a hopper, heated until they become molten and then forced into pre-formed metal moulds. This may produce numbers of either whole beads or half beads which are subsequently glued together. Although the beads are mass-produced, the initial process of creating the mould requires great skill and artistry. Firstly the bead is designed and drawn and then the metal is inscribed and hollowed out with the rough shape. Depending on how complex the design is there may be a number of subsequent carvings before the required degree of fine detail is achieved. The finished die is then used to stamp out the reverse shape and a number of copies are made under great pressure. These are then mounted in moulds which are assembled in two halves to form the shape of the beads.

When sufficiently cool, the beads are released from the moulds, further cooled in tanks of water, then broken from the linking plastic 'branches' which form in the channels of the moulds. These are then tumbled to get rid of any excess plastic or rough edges. Although the bead is now finished, it is often treated further – coated with another 'skin' of colour which may be partially rubbed away to give a two-tone effect or it is given a metallic coating or an iridescent lustre.

Polymer clay

One of the most exciting recent developments in plastics for bead lovers is a variant of polyvinyl chloride known as polymer 'clay'. This is a craft material marketed under various brand names such as 'Fimo', 'Sculpey', 'Cernit' and 'Formello'. It is a plastic compound which comes in a wide range of colours which can be mixed together and is softened by the heat of the hands to a malleable consistency for modelling. It is then hardened by baking in a domestic oven. Polymer clay is the perfect medium for the artistically gifted amateur, unable to afford the expense of kilns, clays and glazes. More than just a child's toy, such exquisite beads and sculptures have been created in the material, that it is now respected as an artistic medium in its own right, not simply a cheaper form of ceramic.

Below Beads with geometric, abstract pattern and pictorial representations, some imitating glass millefiori beads and Islamic folded beads (purple, blue and terracotta)

techniques

chapter six

Materials and Findings

Materials

The next few pages show all the tools, findings and other accessories used for bead jewellery. You may not necessarily need all of them so have a look and decide which are the most appropriate for your purposes.

Round-nosed pliers (1) for making smooth, neat loops in wire.

Snipe-nosed pliers (2) for gripping, opening and closing wire loops on clasps and jump rings etc.

Blunt-nosed pliers (3) for holding flat coils of wire with wide, smooth inner jaws – they cause least marking of the wire.

Wire cutters (4) for cutting wire and tigertail.

An awl (5) is used for tightening knots close to beads, loosening knots, for cleaning out blocked holes and widening holes in wood, bone and clay beads.

Tweezers (6) are used for drawing knots close to beads particularly when thread is used doubled, and for picking up small beads and stones which are difficult to handle.

Fine nail scissors/sharp craft knives (7) are used for cutting thread.

A necklace planner board is made of plastic or wood with one or more curved grooves marked off in inches. It is used for planning the design of a necklace before stringing.

A tape measure (8) is used for checking lengths i.e. pattern repeats, in order to calculate the number of beads required.

Threading material for stringing the beads. A variety of materials are available on the market now – fine nylon, polyester, silk, thick cords, elastic, leather, tigertail, chain and wire.

Beeswax/candles (11) prevent fine thread from tangling – rub thread over the wax before and during use.

Beading needles are fine with a certain degree of flexibility, ranging in length from an average sewing needle to extra long for rocailles threading.

BEAD DESIGN BOARD

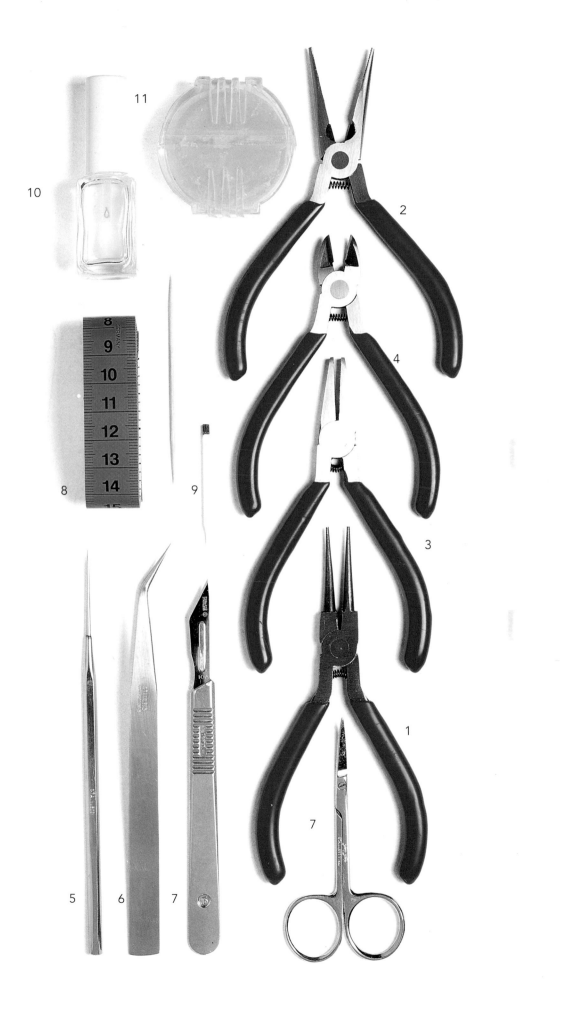

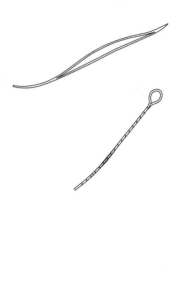

Big eye needles are long, fine, split needles which are very easy to thread (a great advantage for the short-sighted and the ham-fisted!)

Wire bead threaders are made from twisted wire in a variety of thicknesses. The ultra-fine are used for threading semi-precious beads and freshwater pearls which have tiny holes. The wire bead threader is very useful – it is barely thicker than the thread as the loop flattens when it is pulled through the beads. It is also extremely flexible – essential when having to double back through beads.

Home-made threaders are made by twisting together the ends of a piece of fine wire or gimp. Take about an inch of gimp, gently pull it straight, double it and twist into a single length. It is always a good idea to keep a little gimp or fine wire handy just in case your needle breaks – quite simply pass the wire through the loop of the thread and twist into a needle.

A rocailles threader is a gadget with a long, curved needle used especially for threading long strings of rocailles (small embroidery beads). It consists of a plastic bowl and a base with a central pivot; the bowl is filled with rocailles and placed on the pivot. The needle is held with its point in the beads against the curve of the bowl which is then spun and a long line of beads is forced up the needle.

Clear glue/nail polish (10) are used to seal knots. However, never use super glue as it penetrates the thread causing it to become brittle and possibly break.

Cocktail stick/sharpened match stick (9) to assist in applying glue.

Super glue/gum arabic for stiffening the end of thread so that it can be used as a 'needle'.

Jewellers' cement/two-part epoxy resin (Araldite) for gluing cabochons (flat-backed stones) to metal mounts. Jewellers' cement has the advantage of drying absolutely clear. My advice when gluing heavy glass to flat metal mounts is to glue a scrap of fabric to the metal. Allow this to dry before gluing the glass to the fabric.

Tip   Stick sharp ends of needles, awls, knife blades etc. into corks when not in use.

Findings

Clasps are used on necklaces shorter than 61 cm (24") and are always used for bracelets unless they are made from elastic or pre-formed wire.

1 Screw clasp	2 Box clasp	3 Hook and eye clasp
4 Snake clasp	5 Necklace shortener	6 Bolt ring and jump ring
7 Triple box clasp		

Calottes/crimps are used for concealing end knots and/or attaching necklace thread to clasps.

8 Side opening calottes	9 Clamshell calotte	10 Leather calotte
11 Crimps	12 Gimp	

End caps – conical, cylindrical or half spheres are used particularly in multi-stranded necklaces to hide the finishing knots.

13 Conical	14 Half spheres

Bead caps are placed either side of some of the beads in a necklace for emphasis.
15 Metal 'caps' (plain or decorated)

Wire rings

16 Jump rings are made of wire formed into a circular or oval shape and are soldered closed or left open for use as linking rings

17 Split rings are continuous double circles of wire (coiled as in a key ring) which are safer than a single, open ring.

18 Triangles/bails are used as links for attaching pendants to a chain or hook.

19 Spacers/separator bars/hangers have one or more rings at either end. They may be used in both necklaces and earrings to provide a decorative and functional means of separating beads or strings of beads which are then linked to clasps or earhooks. Using jump rings allows them to hang more freely.

Findings for pierced ears are available in precious metal or plated metals.

20 Kidney wire	21 Continental clip	22 Stud and scroll back
23 Ball hooks	24 Hoop	25 Post with mount for stones

Findings for non-pierced ears are generally only available in plated metals.
26 Earclips and earscrews with loops to suspend droppers
27 Earclips and earscrews with mounts for flat backed stones

Pins are pre-cut, shaped lengths of wire threaded with beads to make droppers.
28 Headpins have a small 'head' at the bottom to prevent beads falling off.
29 Eyepins are finished with an 'eye' or loop to which further links can be attached.

chapter seven

Threading

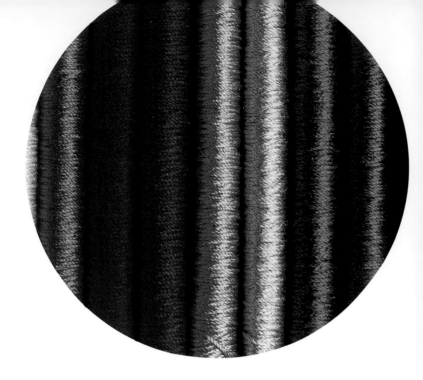

The same method of threading is employed for both necklaces and bracelets. Choose a suitable clasp for the size, weight and colour of the beads but remember that bracelet clasps have to be manipulated with one hand so box or spring clasps are preferable to screw clasps.

Materials

The kind of threading material is determined by both the size of the hole in the beads and their weight. If the hole is small, a fine thread is needed but if the hole is small and the bead is heavy, the thread must not only be fine, but also strong.

Silk comes in a wide range of colours and thicknesses. It was traditionally used for stringing pearls or semi-precious beads as its high lustre and suppleness enable it to slide easily through the beads without tangling, ensuring that they hang gracefully. Silk is available wound onto card in lengths of approximately two metres (sufficient for a long necklace) with an attached twisted wire needle, or in longer lengths wound onto small spools.

Man-made fibres rival silk for richness of colour and have the added advantage of strength even when very fine (the thinner gauges of silk are liable to break more easily). *Polyester thread* can come with a waxed finish which enables it to pass more easily through the beads and prevents tangling. You can do this yourself by rubbing unwaxed thread over a candle or beeswax. *Bonded nylon* in fine gauges is the least prone both to tangling and stretching and is therefore suitable for all types of beads.

Leather thonging, cotton or polyester lacing are both useful and decorative for large-holed ceramic, glass or wooden beads particularly when a single bead is threaded for dramatic effect.

Elastic is used for lightweight beads with fairly large holes. It is particularly useful for stringing childrens' necklaces and bracelets without having to use a clasp.

Tigertail (a strong, nylon-coated wire) is sometimes used when threading a mix of heavy-weight beads and those with sharp edges, particularly metal which may cut through ordinary thread. It is not recommended for most beads because of its tendency to kink and without a certain amount of weight the necklace will hang awkwardly. A necklace threaded on tigertail will never have the sensuous, fluid feel of one that is strung on more supple materials.

Nylon monofilament (clear plastic line used for fishing) is possibly the worst material of all for bead stringing. Not only does it kink badly when used with lightweight beads, it also stretches considerably when carrying heavy beads and even worse, it is very difficult to make a decent knot. It is, however, useful for quick threading to plan a necklace or bracelet as it does not require a needle. The finer gauges are sometimes used in bead weaving when a visible thread may look obtrusive.

Tip All types of thread will stretch in time though bonded nylon has the least stretch. The best way to combat stretching is either to hang the thread with a weight on it before threading or to hang the necklace for a few hours before finishing it off. Whichever thread you choose, and whether using single, double or multiple strands, you should use the thickest that will pass easily through the beads, as too much movement causes friction, subsequent fraying and snapping of the thread. On the other hand, the needle and thread should never be forced through the beads as this will result in the breakage of needle, thread or bead.

Preparations

Before you start threading make sure your working area is uncluttered. It is best to work on a piece of velvet or felt (or any soft cloth with a close pile) which provide a fairly clingy surface: use a plain colour so that the beads are easily visible. A necklace design board is very useful for laying the beads out in order. Alternatively, fold your cloth into grooves or use plasticene or polymer clay to make a more fixed groove to hold the beads – roll it into a long 'sausage', mould a groove and bend it into a curve. Keep all surplus beads in shallow but stable containers that will not tip over easily and make sure all your tools and findings are within easy reach. You should always work in good light as many of the components used are very small and needle threading requires good visibility both for the sake of eyesight and temper!

Finishing necklaces and bracelets

Temporary knot

A slip knot is tied in the thread before stringing to prevent the beads from falling off. This is easily undone by pulling the loose end.

Finishing knots

Necklaces that will fit over your head do not need a clasp and may be finished in the following ways.

Method a

The single reef knot (square knot) is a neat way of finishing the two ends of the necklace. This knot will sit at the back of the neck in the centre. Allow at least an extra 15 cm (6 in) to tie the knot. Make a slip knot in the thread and string on all the beads in the desired pattern. Undo the slip knot, then follow the diagrams:

  1 Take end B and pass it over and under end A.

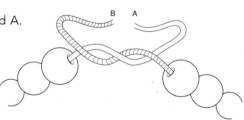

  2 Again, take end B and pass it over and under end A.

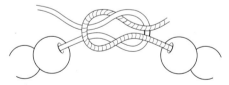

  3 Pull both ends carefully until knot tightens. Pull out both loops of the knot until the beads are drawn close together as the knot is tightened.

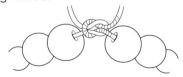

  4 Apply a little glue or clear nail polish to the knot and allow to dry.
  5 Either snip the ends neatly with nail scissors or thread them into the few adjacent beads and trim.

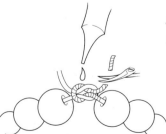

Method b

Knots are made either side of a few central beads which allows the necklace to sit smoothly on the back of the neck. Allow about 30 cm (12") extra thread for making the knots. The thread must be fine enough to pass twice through some of the beads and a flexible wire threader should be used, rather than a rigid needle. Firstly make a slip knot and string on the three beads which will be at the centre back, followed by the rest of the beads in the desired pattern. Undo the slip knot then follow the diagrams:

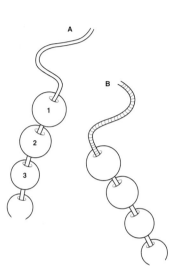

1 Take end B and pass it through the first three beads on end A.
2 Even up the amounts of spare thread either side of the three centre beads.
3 Pull ends A and B until all the beads are drawn close together but not too tightly as there must be sufficient slack to allow for two knots either side of the middle three beads.

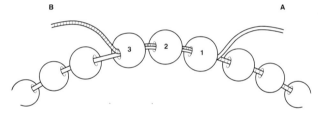

4 Take end B and make a knot over thread A close to bead **3**, then pass it through the next bead.

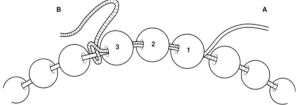

5 Knot end A over thread B close to bead **1** then pass it through the next bead.

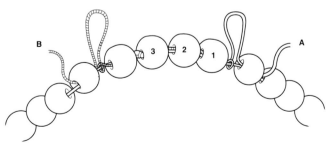

6 Make one more knot as before on either side and pass both ends through the adjacent beads.
7 Apply a drop of glue to each of the knots to seal them.
8 Trim ends A and B close to the beads.

Finishing with clasps

Necklaces that do not fit over your head require clasps. Most clasps, whether they are screw, spring, box, single or multiple strand, have loops for attaching them to the string of beads. The means by which they are attached – calottes, bead tips and gimp – usually depends on the material on which the beads are threaded.

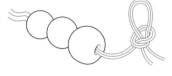

Slip knot

Single overhand knot

Double overhand knot

Side opening calottes are available in two sizes – small for fine to medium gauges of thread and large for the heavier gauges and thin cord. Their advantage over clamshell calottes and bead tips is that they may be put on after the necklace has been entirely strung. Any mistakes in threading can be easily rectified and adjustments to the length may be made before fixing them over the finishing knots.

Method

If possible, work with a doubled strand of thread, as it is easier to get knots close to the beads. Make a slip knot at the end. Once you have finished threading, undo the slip knot, adjust the length if necessary by adding or removing beads and make an overhand knot at the beginning of the string, leaving a little thread to spare. This knot must be substantial enough not to pull through the notch in the calotte. NB If using a single strand of thread, make a double overhand knot by passing the thread twice through the loop. Apply a little glue or nail polish to the knot and allow to dry.

1 Take a calotte and position the knot in one half so that the necklace thread lies in the notch and the loop of the calotte points away from the beads.

2 Take a pair of pliers and squeeze the two halves of the calotte closed over the knot.

3 Push all the beads up the thread as close as possible against the calotte and make a second knot immediately after the last bead (an awl or tweezers will help get this knot really close). If using a double strand, after making the knot, tighten it closer to the beads by pulling the two threads away from each other.

4 Seal the knot with a drop of glue.

5 Put on the second calotte in the same manner as the first.

6 Trim the ends of thread as closely to the calottes as possible.

7 Using a pair of pliers, open up the loops of the calottes by gently twisting them sideways, hook them into the rings of the clasp and then squeeze them closed.

Clamshell calottes and bead tips are frequently made in precious metals and are often used for semi-precious and finer quality beads. They tend to have smaller holes than the side opening calotte and may be used with finer threads. Clamshell calottes or bead tips cannot be put on after the finishing knots are made so it is preferable to have the design and final length of the necklace worked out before you even start threading. Use a double strand of thread for stringing as it is easier to get the final knot close into the calotte or bead tip.

Method

1 Make an overhand knot, leaving a small tail of thread.
2 Seal the knot with glue.
3 Take a clamshell or bead tip and thread it so that the knot is on the inside.
4 If using the clamshell, close it up with pliers, and trim off the excess thread.
5 Thread on all the beads and push them as far as possible up the thread.
6 Take your second calotte or bead tip and pass it on to the thread.
7 Make a knot, using an awl or tweezers to draw it as tightly as possible into the bead tip or calotte. When using a double thread, cut off the needle and take each of the two ends of thread and pull gently but firmly outwards. This draws the knot closer into the bead tip or clamshell (see below).
8 Seal with glue as before.
9 Close up the clamshell with pliers, and trim off the excess thread.
10 Attach the loops of the calottes or bead tips to the necklace clasp.

Tip Another way of keeping the second clamshell tightly against the beads is to thread on a bead small enough to be contained inside it. Then, make the final knot and close the calotte over bead and knot. Take care not to force the calotte to close too tightly or you may break the bead inside.

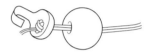

Bead tip

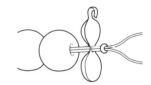

Clamshell calotte

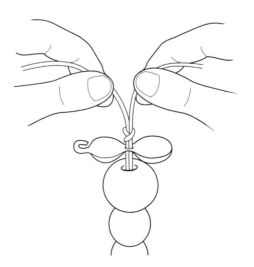

Gimp ends are made from very fine, flexible, coiled wire tubing and are used to reinforce the necklace thread at the points where it is looped through the rings of the necklace clasp. It is a technique worth mastering as the knots of fine thread can pull through the holes of the calottes and gimp is what you need in this instance. It is preferable to have the design of the necklace finalized, and the beads laid out ready in the order of threading. As the thread has to pass twice through the first and last three beads on the string, the holes of these beads must be large enough.

Method a

1 Make a slip knot at the end of the thread, leaving a spare tail.
2 Thread on the first three beads.
3 Pass the needle and thread through a piece of gimp.
4 Take one half of the clasp and pass the needle, thread and gimp end through the ring, taking care not to damage the gimp.

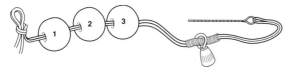

5 Pass the needle back through bead **3** and carefully draw the thread taut until the gimp curls into a rounded loop against the bead.

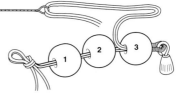

6 Make a half-hitch knot after bead **3** and then pass the needle and thread through bead **2**.

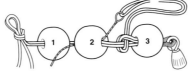

7 Make a half-hitch knot after bead **2** and pass needle and thread through bead **1**.

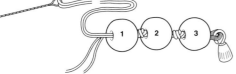

8 Undo the slip knot, and use this spare end of thread to make a half-hitch knot over the necklace thread after bead **1**.

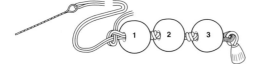

9 Seal this knot with a little glue and trim away the spare thread.
10 Thread on the rest of the beads, pushing them as close together as possible. Allow a small amount of play in the last four beads as you are going to knot between these.
11 Repeat the knotting process outlined above, adjusting the thread so that there is just enough space for the knots, making sure that no gaps appear between knots and beads.
12 Make a final knot over the necklace thread after bead **1**, seal with glue and trim away the spare end.

Method b

When using ultra-fine thread follow this alternative method which requires only one set of knots to be made at one end of the strand. Three beads (to be used at the end) must have holes large enough to take six thicknesses of thread.

1 Pass both ends of a length of thread through a wire bead threader, so that a loop is formed at the other end.
2 Pass a piece of gimp over the needle and down the thread towards this loop, followed by one half of the clasp.

3 Pass the needle through the loop of thread.

4 Pull taut and coil the gimp around the clasp ring, then thread on all the beads except for the last three reserved beads.

5 Thread on the last three beads, a piece of gimp and the second half of the clasp.
6 Finish in the same way as described in the first method.

Finishing multi-strand necklaces

Some large calottes will take a number of threads but if you cannot get hold of these, there are alternative ways of finishing this type of necklace.

Method a (end caps)

1 Knot all threads close to the beads

2 Make a second knot, but before pulling it tight, hook either the loop of an eyepin or a piece of wire through the knot, pull tight, seal with glue and trim off the thread ends.

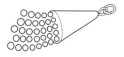

3 Thread the wire through the hole of the end cap and cut, leaving sufficient spare (at least 8 mm) to make a loop with round-nosed pliers, which will not pull back through the end cap.

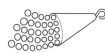

4 Add a jump ring to provide a link for the necklace clasp.

Method b (small calottes)

1 Knot all the threads close to the beads and seal with glue. Trim away all but about two or three strands.
2 Thread these through an end cap.

3 Make a knot close to the cap and seal with glue.
4 Fix a calotte over the knot.

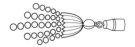

5 Add a necklace clasp with loops or a jump ring.

Method c

In order to join a multi-strand necklace to a single strand, follow these instructions:

1 Finish the multi-strand necklace in the manner described in **Method b (calottes)** as far as Step 2, cutting off all threads but those needed for the single strand.

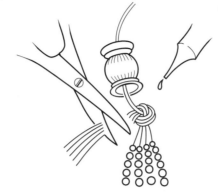

2 Thread on an end cap or large-holed bead and slide this over the knot.
3 Thread on the beads for the single strand and finish off appropriately.

Method d

Attach a multi-strand to a single thong or a thick cord by using large calottes linked to a leather calotte or push-in crimp.

Tip A necklace shortener clasp is used with long ropes of small beads as folllows:

1 Thread up long, single strands of small beads – try a mix of different sizes of rocailles and bugles for texture, or magatama (off-centre holed beads) for a pretty, knobbly effect.
2 Make sure the strands are the same length (1 m) and then tie the ends of each in a square (reef) knot.
3 Put a finger through the loops at either end then twist a number of times and secure the twist by linking both loops with a necklace shortener clasp.

Finishing leather and cord with a clasp

To finish leather or thick cord there are two types of calottes – calotte with flaps or the push-in crimp.

Method a (leather calottes)

1 Trim the leather or cord to the desired length.
2 Take a calotte and lay the end of the thonging in it so that the loop is pointing away from the necklace. (Thin leather or cord may be doubled first.)
3 Squeeze one calotte flap over the thonging with pliers until it grips tightly. Test it by tugging gently on the thonging.
4 Squeeze the second flap over the first.
5 Repeat the process at the other end.
6 Take the clasp and open up the loops by twisting gently sideways.
7 Hook the loops of the clasp into the calotte loops.

Method b (push-in crimp)

1 Push the end of the thong into the crimp.
2 Take a pair of pliers and squeeze the last couple of coils tightly so that it bites into the thonging. Test by tugging gently.

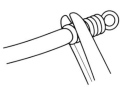

or

1 Squeeze a little glue into the crimp.
2 Push the thonging in and allow to dry.
3 Test by tugging gently.
4 For extra security, the last coil or so may be squeezed tight with the pliers.

Threading with different materials

Leather and thick cord thonging

These are usually used for large-holed or pendant beads; the thonging and knots are part of the overall decorative effect of the necklace. No needles are required for leather or thick cord. However, if the latter is frayed, seal the end with clear glue or nail polish.

Single pendants or beads whose hole goes from front to back (rather than from side to side) may be strung in the following way:

Method

1 Pass both ends of thonging through the hole from the back to the front.
2 Pull both ends through the loop at the front.
3 Pull taut.

When a few beads are threaded to hang in the centre they may be secured in position by tying an overhand knot either side of the group.

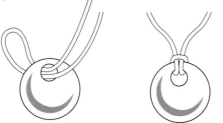

If you finish your necklace with a knot you will need a metre of thonging which can simply be tied in a bow like a shoelace.

Tip Finishing both thonging ends with a bead prevents them being pulled through into a fixed knot and also looks more 'finished'.

There is a useful, adjustable knot for thonging which allows the necklace to be lengthened to go over the head then shortened to an appropriate position. Again, you will need no less than a metre. Thread on your beads and then for the knots, follow these instructions.

Method

1 Centre the beads on the thonging and lay the necklace with the beads away from you.
2 Bring both ends of thonging down towards the beads, end B to the left of thong A.
3 Hold both threads in your right hand in the manner shown, allowing a sufficient amount of end B to make a double knot.
4 Bring end B towards you, over the thumb, and take back under both threads.
5 Repeat this, then pass end B through both the loops on your thumb and pull taut.
6 Turn the necklace over so that end A is to the left of thong B and make a second knot in the same way as the first .
7 Trim the spare ends of thonging neatly.
8 The necklace is lengthened by pushing the knots away from the beads and shortened by pulling them towards the beads.

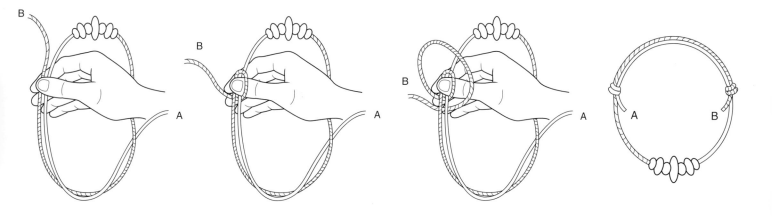

Tip I have used double knots but single knots, although less decorative, are equally functional. Just make one loop over the thumb, pass the thong end through that loop and pull taut.

Tigertail

Use tigertail when threading a mix of heavy beads or sharp-edged beads. It is generally finished with soft brass crimping beads to fix it to the loops of the clasp.

Method

1 Slip a crimp over the tigertail.
2 Pass the tigertail through a loop of the clasp and back through the crimp.
3 Push the crimp close to the clasp and squeeze it tightly with pliers so that the tigertail is firmly secured.

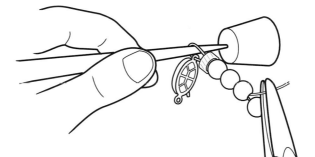

4 Thread on the beads, pushing them over the two thicknesses of tigertail, close to the crimp.

5 To finish off, the same process is repeated at the other end of the necklace. An awl and a pair of pliers will assist in this process. Before threading the tigertail back through the crimp and beads, loop it over an awl which is stuck into a cork.

6 With the pliers, grip the end of the tigertail and pull it through the crimp and beads so that a neat loop is formed round the awl, and the beads are drawn close together.
7 Holding the end of the tigertail so that it remains taut, squeeze the crimp tight, remove the cork from the awl then withdraw the awl from the loop of the tigertail.
8 Trim the tigertail end close to the beads with wire cutters.

Chain

Fine chain may be used for threading beads which are secured in position with crimping beads. For a delicate effect, do this at intervals on the chain by squeezing a crimp either side of a bead or group of beads.

The same effect can be achieved when using a larger chain by first threading the beads on eyepins and making a loop the other end. You then hook the loops into the links of chain sections.

Alternatively, hang clusters of beads linked by jump rings to the chain.

Decorative knotting

Knotting between beads

Knotting separates and cushions fragile, delicate beads. If the thread breaks (all threads are subject to wear and tear), most of the beads are kept safe. In addition, knotting with a toning or contrasting thread often enhances the beads, emphasizing an unusual shape or colour. If you are knotting between each bead in a necklace, allow approximately three times more thread than the required finished length.

Single strand (double overhand knot)

When using a single strand (braided thick silk or cord), a double knot sits better than a single knot. It is fairly tricky to keep both loops in the thread apart until they have come close to the bead and a pair of fine tweezers or an awl, withdrawn at the last moment when the knot coils against the bead is most helpful.

Double strand (single overhand knot)

It is by far easier to get the knot close to the beads by using a double strand of thread, and by making a single overhand knot. Use tweezers or an awl to assist. Finally, take each strand between the thumb and forefinger of each hand and pull them away from each other to further tighten the knot (see page 59).

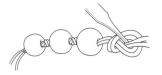

Expensive beads knotted at intervals on toning coloured thread looks pretty and also uses fewer costly beads. For a double row of beads, use two strands of silk with their own needle. Make an overhand knot at the end, then separate the strands and knot a bead on each, either so the beads lie parallel to each other or slightly overlap. The knotted necklace can be finished in any of the ways outlined previously.

For beads wth larger holes the following knots make a decorative way of finishing off a necklace. A loop and bead closure can be used as an integral part of the necklace. Use heavy silk or cord of a suitable thickness and allow plenty of thread. Before you start threading the beads, anchor the thread at one end around a pencil to keep the correct tension between the knots.

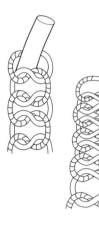

Method a

Loop the thread around a pencil or dowel, make a series of square (reef) knots, pulling evenly to tighten the knots. The first loop acts as the loop of the necklace closure. Once you have completed threading, finish off the other end with a bead and a sealed knot. For an open effect keep alternate loops open between knots.

Method b

Four strands can be used for a more sumptuous, bulky look. To help keep track of the pattern, mark the right hand outer thread B with nail polish – this thread is always the one which passes through the loop. Start by knotting the two outer strands over the two inner (these can be shorter as they do not do any work).

1 Take the left outer thread A across and over the inner threads, and under thread B on the right.
2 Bring end B across and under the inner threads and out through the loop thus formed.
3 Take end A across and over the inner threads and under end B on the left.
4 Bring end B across and under the inner threads and out through the loop thus formed.

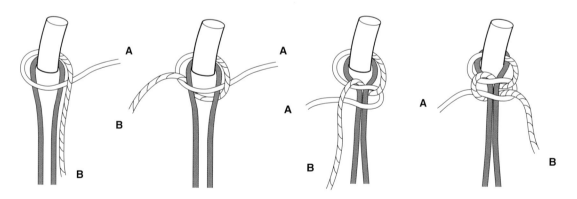

A double loop closure may be bound with fine silk of the same colour either with a button-hole stitch or bind both strands with figure of eight loops, taking the thread over and under the strand each time as you move to and fro. Tuck the spare ends of thread between the strands. Once you have completed threading, finish off the other end with a bead and a sealed knot.

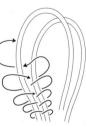

Decorative threading

Looped effects

Necklaces with decorative loops of beads are formed by taking back the thread to pass a second time through one or more of the beads on the necklace strand.

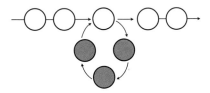

Working with two or more needles enables you to combine two or more rows of beads with a single row to create a lacy, open-work effect. To combine double rows of beads with single rows, use two working strands each with its own needle. Both needles and threads are joined together to pass through a single row, then separated out to thread two separate rows.

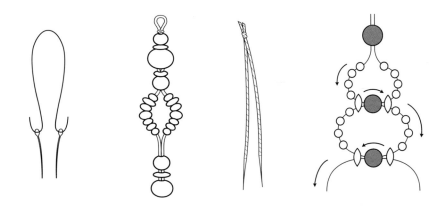

Alternatively, join the rows closely together by combining large beads with small ones. A double row of large beads with a triple row of small beads are strung on a toning thread (see the Square Knot and Glass Bead Collar on page 90).

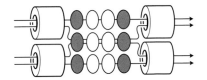

Off-loom weaving

There are many weaving patterns for beaded jewellery which can be achieved without using a loom. The following designs are some of the simplest yet are very effective.

The types of beads most commonly used for bead weaving are rocailles, embroidery beads or small round beads, usually no larger than 5 mm. These are generally sold in small plastic bottles or packs, usually weighing between 5 and 20 grams. As a rough guide for a 10 gm pack:

Size 8/0	approx. 300 beads	85 cm (33 1/2") length
Size 11/0	approx. 1000 beads	140 cm (55 1/8") length
Size 3''' bugles	approx. 130 beads	185 cm (72 3/4") length

Rocailles round in shape are made in sizes generally ranging from 12/0 to 5/0; the higher the size number, the smaller the bead. Bugle beads, small fine tubes, are sized the other way round: the greater the number the longer the length – size 1''' is approx. 3 mm (1/8") long, size 3''' approx. 9 mm (3/8").

Generally speaking, the more expensive the rocailles and bugles, the more regular is the sizing, both of the outer measurement and of the hole. When using the beads for weaving, it is important that they are regular in size. Unfortunately rocailles sizings are not standardized from one manufacturer to another so it is better not to mix the sources of supply.

Embroidery beads come in a bewildering variety of colours, many enhanced or intensified with rainbow, pearly or metallic finishes or with a coloured or silver lining. These coatings vary in their degree of permanence, so its worth checking this before starting a project, either with the suppliers or, by doing a test: soak some of the beads to be used in a solution of bleach. It is best to buy more beads than are actually needed, as different batches vary in colour.

Materials
Strong, fine thread (preferably polyester or bonded nylon)
Fine beading needle
Candle or beeswax
Beads sorted into sizes

Tip   It is best not to work with too long a thread – if you run out, knot on a fresh length using a square knot, seal with glue and conceal inside the beads, or if possible, pass a fresh length through some of the beads already threaded, without making any knots.

Open daisy chain

This is a delicate open daisy chain formed by separating the 'flower' with one or more beads in between.

Method

1 Thread on two beads.
2 Start the daisy by threading beads **1, 2, 3, 4, 5,** into the centre bead **6,** back through bead **1,** through beads **7, 8, 9,** back through bead **5** and pull taut to make the daisy shape.
3 Thread on 2 more beads and repeat the daisy sequence as many times as necessary.

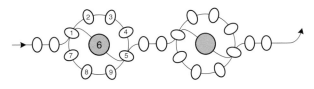

Closed daisy chain

The closed daisy chain is firmer and more solid in effect as the flowers are joined together without any linking beads.

Method

The threading pattern starts in the same way, but after bead **9,** passes once more through bead **5,** then beads **10, 11,** back through **9,** back through **10,** into **12** etc. Repeat this sequence as many times as necessary.

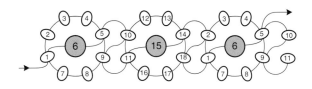

Finish off in the conventional way with a metal clasp. Alternatively, after the last daisy, pass the thread back through the beads and pulling tight, knot the spare end firmly over the necklace thread. Rethread the spare end at the beginning, add sufficient beads to make a loop over the last daisy and knot the end as before over the necklace thread.

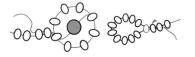

Lacy stitch

This is a design to make lacy, open-work collars which lie at the base of the throat. The more repeats of the pattern you do on the downward strand before turning back, the longer the fringes of the collar will be. The collars can be made from beads of one colour but the pattern is easier to follow without counting if you use toning colours or beads in a slightly larger size (indicated by shading in the line drawing) – these are the linking beads which form the lacy pattern.

Method

1 Leave plenty of thread at the beginning for finishing off the collar.
2 When threading, follow the direction of the arrows to see the order in which the beads are strung.
3 Do as many pattern repeats as necessary to reach the length you require.

4 When the piece is completed it may be finished off with a metal clasp, gimp ends or calottes or with a closure of loop and bead. See previous page for instructions.

chapter eight

Wire

The other major threading material used in bead jewellery is wire. All pins and wires should be cut with wire cutters and never with scissors. To make neat loops, round-nosed pliers should be used, whereas blunt- or snipe-nosed pliers are better for opening and closing loops as they grip the wire more efficiently. There are available preformed wire shapes which have specific uses – these are described below.

Wire pins

Headpins are used to make droppers for earrings. They have a small stopper at the end to prevent the beads from falling off. Headpins are threaded with beads to the required length (if the head of the pin is too small to restrain the beads, first thread on a small bead or bead cap), then the wire is cut to allow sufficient spare to make a neat round loop (about 8 mm). Position the wire between the pliers, not too close to the points so that the cut end of the wire is flush with the top rounded edges. Grasping firmly, bend the wire over the curve of the pliers, using a rolling motion. Just before the loop meets the straight wire, rock the loop back so that it becomes rounded and centred at the end of the wire rather than 'p' shaped. Slide the loop closer to the points of the pliers to complete a neat closure. The threaded pin is then hung from an earhook.

When opening up loops in wire or wire jump rings, always twist the wire gently sideways, never force the ends away from each other as this will put too much stress on the loop and cause it to break.

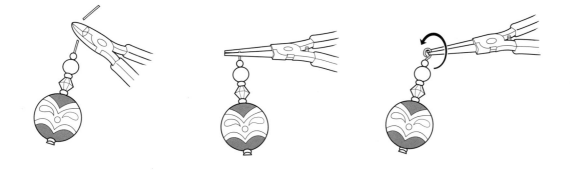

Eyepins are used in a similar way but they are more versatile as the pin has a loop so that you can hang a pendant bead. They can also be used to join together a number of components: groups of beads, spacers or sections of chain.

When making the loop at the other end of the eyepin, consider which way you want the attachment to lie. Note that in the line drawing below the final loop is made at right angles to the first, so that the star faces to the front when the eyepin is hooked into the spacer-hanger.

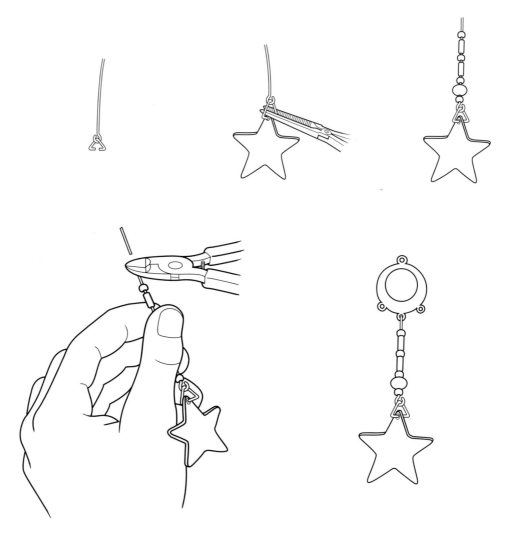

In this line drawing, where the pin links two spacers, the loops lie in the same direction. Loops should always be fashioned like this and not somewhere in between which will look messy.

Tip When making a number of identical components (the beads must be the same size), cut all the pins needed to the same length. Thread the beads onto the pin and cut the wire to the correct length. Do not discard the waste end, but use either this or the pin itself as a measure to cut the other pins to length.

Jump rings are useful small links for joining a number of head/eyepins or sections of chain together. The oval is better than the round shape as it lies flatter. Opening and closing jump rings, which are often made of hard wire, is made easier by using two pairs of pliers, using a sideways twisting motion.

Triangular links/bails are used when the pendant is too thick to fit inside the curvature of a round or oval jump ring.

Split ring This is a continuous double circle of wire like a miniature key ring. Its use is similar to that of a jump ring but offers greater security as it is not easily forced open.

Preformed wire coil

Toughened wire coil, sold in two sizes for bracelet and necklace collars, is available from specialist shops. This can be cut into single or multiple coils of two or more and threaded with beads. The wire is formed into a neat loop at one end, threaded with beads and then finished with a loop at the other end. As the wire keeps its shape there is no need for a clasp. Also available are single wire coils with bead stoppers (one bead unscrews so that you can thread your choice of beads onto the coil).

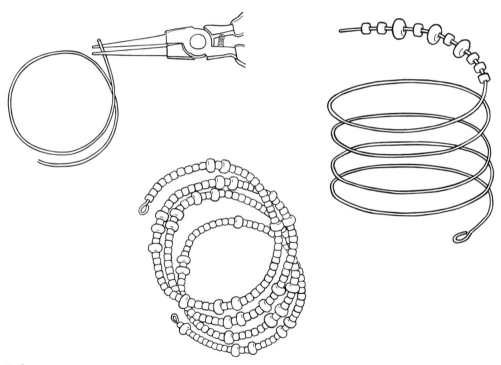

Safety pins

Safety pins threaded with beads and then strung together create a stunning effect. When strung through the coil of the pin, as the bottoms are fatter than the tops, the string will lie in a curve; to make the curve more gradual, space the pins with a bead. See project on page 108.

Stick pins

These pins which have a sharpened point and a protector cap usually have a flat front onto which a flat shape is glued, to make a lapel pin.

Hat pins

These are long pins with a sharpened point and a removable safety cap which also helps anchor the pin. Some pins have a head to restrain the beads, others do not, and must be formed into a loop. When they are threaded with beads, a crimping bead is squeezed onto the wire to keep them in position. A little glue is applied as the crimp is fixed to increase security. These hatpins can also be used as dramatic lapel pins.

Using wire to make your own findings

Wire is more versatile than pre-cut pins or jump rings and it is frequently used for decorative effect. It may be hard or soft, according to how it has been annealed, but generally, the thinner the wire, the easier it is to manipulate; the thicker it is, the more likely it is to keep its shape once bent into position. Wire comes in various gauges and finishes – the finer the wire, the more flexible it is. For coils that need to keep their shape, use 0.6 mm up to 1.2 mm thicknesses; whilst thinner wires than these are best for decorative wrapping. Wire of 1 mm or thicker is used to make rigid hoops for necklaces and bracelets. Wire is available in copper, brass, silver and gold plate on copper, sold either by the weight or length. Gold and sterling silver wire are available from bullion merchants.

The tools you will need for working with wire are cutters, round-nosed pliers for making loops, and snipe-nosed and blunt-nosed pliers for gripping the wire firmly while coiling or shaping it. Great care should be taken when bending wire, as once this has been done, unless the wire is very soft, it is often impossible to remove the kinks. To make curves in wire, wrap it round a rigid cylindrical object and smooth it with your fingers (a dowel for small curves - useful for earrings; a broom handle for bracelet curves and a bottle or a cylindrical vase for a wire neck collar).

**Hook and eye clasp
Single strand**

**Hook and eye clasp
Double strand**

Front fastener with linking rings

'S'-shaped necklace closure using jump rings (the bead is fixed by a crimp bead)

Toggle for thick cord or leather

Pendant findings
Wire can be used to hang beads or pendants that are pierced horizontally across the apex.

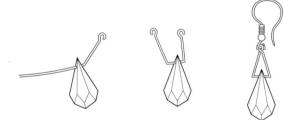

Coils
Make coils by starting the curve around a dowel, then with the tips of snipe-nosed pliers make a tight curl at the centre. Grip flat with blunt-nosed pliers whilst tightening the coils.

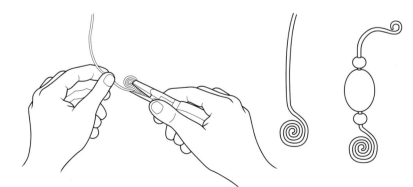

Loops for earrings

You can make both round and teardrop-shaped loops. For the latter, pull the wire coil down at the centre bottom.

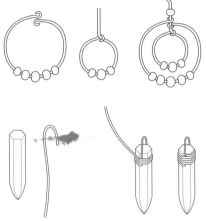

Unpierced crystal (0.6 mm wire)

Irregularly-shaped, pierced nugget (0.4 mm wire)

If the nugget is not pierced, bind with wire first and finish by twisting into a loop.

Knitted beaded shapes (0.35 mm)

These are made with very fine copper wire. You need only knit two or three rows with beads then the last two or three can be either decreased or the spare wire passed through a row of stitches. Because of the nature of the wire, the finished piece may be easily bent into shape to disguise any irregularities – but if you want to make two similar shapes for earrings, keep a note of the pattern so that you can repeat it.

Coil-wrapped round beads (0.6 mm wire)

Use a dowel to make curves to fit around the bead.

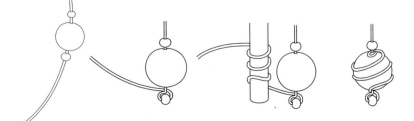

Pierced front clips for beading

These findings provide an alternative means of matching accessories to your necklace. The clasp may be worn either at the back of the necklace or as a feature at the front. The metal front which is pierced with holes at regular intervals is clipped onto the back of the finding by means of lugs which are bent over with pliers. The beads are attached either with thread, nylon monofilament or fine wire.

Earclips, clasps and brooches

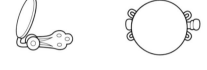

The pierced front clips on to earclip or a two-row necklace clasp.

The pierced oval front clips on to oval brooch back.

Method

1 Start by knotting the thread at the back (or if using wire, twist the ends at the back).
2 Thread on the centre bead, take needle and thread through to the back, then bring up to the front to start the next row.

3 Thread on sufficient beads to complete the next row, curling them around the central bead, and take the thread through to the back.

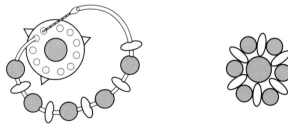

4 Secure this row at intervals by going once more through a few of the beads, down to the back, up again through the next few beads and so on, until the row is fixed in position.
5 Repeat until there is no metal visible.

Oval fittings are worked in the same way, but the beads will lie more evenly if you put either an oval bead or a row of beads at the centre.

Beaded hairclips

These are flat metal or plastic hairclips with a hole at each end for single, double or multiple row beading. Use either needle and toning thread, nylon monofilament or wire to attach the beads (thread is more flexible, particularly when stringing two or more rows).

If beading on wire, the wire is passed through the holes at either end of the clip and bent into loops to secure the beads in position. If beading on thread, you will need to use beads as stoppers, either toning metal beads, or ones which match the others you are using. These should be large enough so as not to pass through the holes of the clip but small enough to be unobtrusive. They should have fairly large holes if the thread is to pass through them more than once.

Method

To make a two-row beaded clip you will need 4 stopper beads and sufficient beads for the double row.

 1 Start with a slip knot at the end of the thread.
 2 Thread on a stopper bead **1** and take the needle through the hole at one end of the clip from the back to the front.
 3 Thread on a stopper bead **2**.
 4 Thread on sufficient beads to lie neatly along the clip, finishing with a stopper bead **3**.
 5 Pass the needle and thread through the hole at the other end.
 6 Thread on the stopper bead **4**, pull the thread taut and take the needle back through the hole and the stopper bead **3**.
 7 Thread on the second row of beads, go back through the stopper bead **2** and the hole at the end.
 8 Undo the slip knot, and take the needle and thread through the stopper bead **1**.
 9 Remove the needle and tie both ends of thread tightly together.
10 Seal the knot and trim away the spare thread.

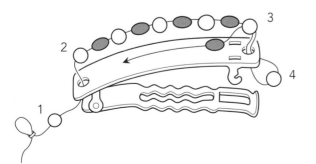
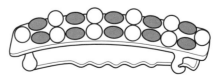

projects

Triple-Thong Necklace and Earrings

This triple-row choker may be threaded on either leather or cotton thonging. The beads used here are tea-dyed bone with red-stained horn and gold-plated plastic spacers. When choosing the beads, make sure the holes are large enough to take the thickness of the thonging. No special techniques are needed for this project; the beads are simply threaded and the thong tied with a basic overhand knot. The earrings are also threaded on thonging, the ends of which are joined with leather calottes and attached to the earfittings. For cutting the leather, you will need wire cutters or heavy scissors.

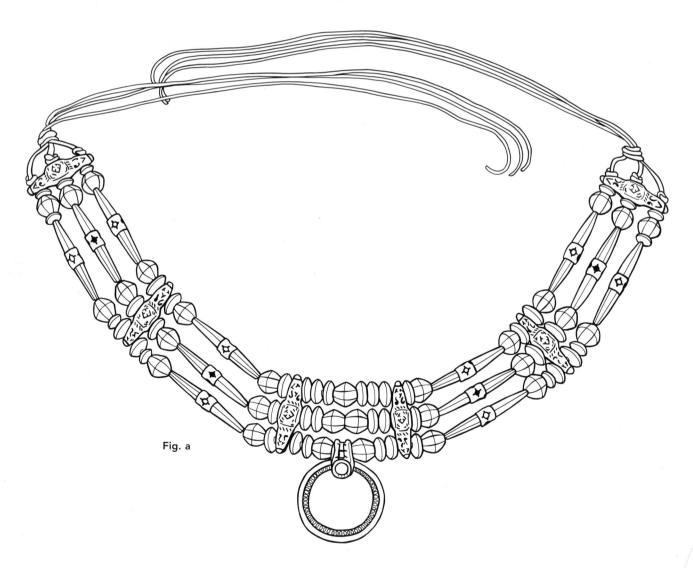

Fig. a

Necklace

Materials

6 x 3-holed gold-plated plastic spacers

29 x 8 mm red-stained horn beads (shaded on **Fig. a**)

12 long bone beads

32 x 10 mm bone discs

12 x 6 mm bone discs

1 large gold-plated plastic pendant

3 m approx. thin leather thong or cotton lacing

Instructions

Please note that the lengths of the rows increase gradually from top to bottom to enable the necklace to sit comfortably at the base of the neck. If you want to wear it higher, omit the 6 extra 6 mm bone discs on the bottom.

1 Look carefully at **Fig. a** before starting to thread. The first two rows are threaded in the same way except for the centre section between the two middle spacers. The bottom row has more changes – it has 3 small discs inserted at intervals, either side of the middle section.

Centre section

Row 1	3 large discs	1 red bead	3 large discs		
Row 2	2 large discs	2 red beads	2 large discs		
Row 3	2 large discs	1 red bead	1 pendant	1 red bead	2 large discs

2 Start to thread the thong, according to **Fig. a**. Adjust the beads on the thonging so that there are equal amounts of thong either side of the three rows.
3 On each of the three rows, make an overhand knot after each end spacer, carefully pulling the beads together as you do so.
4 Gather the three thongs together either side of the necklace, and make an overhand knot close to the three single knots.
5 Finally trim the ends of the thongs so that they are of equal length.
6 The necklace is closed by simply tying at the back with a knot. A reef (square) knot is the most comfortable.

Earrings

Materials

6 x 10 mm gold-plated plastic beads, large hole (to take 2 thicknesses of thong)

6 x 8 mm red-stained horn beads (shaded on **Figs. b & c**)

4 x 10 mm bone discs

4 x 6 mm bone discs

2 x leather calottes

1 pair gold-coloured earfitting

2 x 16 cm lengths of thin leather thong or cotton lacing

Instructions

1 Divide the beads into two piles, one for each earring.
2 Take one length of thonging, and thread on 1 gold bead.
3 Add the rest of the beads according to **Fig. b**.
4 Pass the end of the thonging back through the first gold bead.
5 Lay the two ends of thonging in a leather calotte, adjusting the length to suit you.
6 With pliers, squeeze first one flap of the calotte over the thong ends, then the second flap over the first.
7 Hang the earring from the earfitting (see **Fig. c**).
8 Complete the second earring in the same way.

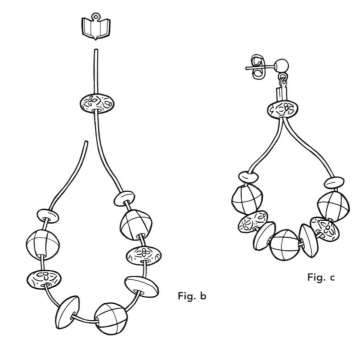

Fig. b

Fig. c

Square Knot and Glass Bead Collar

This two-row choker is threaded on four strands of silk finished in a square knot design. Some of the beads you choose must have holes large enough to take two strands of thread, three of them must take four strands. Look at **Fig. a** before you start threading. As the collar should fit tightly around the neck, it is advisable to do a test run – thread one row of beads to see where they reach on your neck and measure the difference. Divide this measurement into two, which will give you the amount of square knots to be made either side to finish the collar. In the necklace shown, the measurement is 6 cm (2") not including the loop and bead closure which takes up about half an inch. The measurements give an overall length of 38-40 cm (15-16") as the thread has a certain amount of elasticity. For this project you will need super glue, scissors and a tape measure.

Fig. a

Necklace

Materials

10 x 25 mm black glass tubes

11 x 8 mm goldstone glass beads

24 x 6 mm pink glass beads

16 x size 8/0 dull gold rocailles

2 x 2 m cards of medium thickness green silk with attached needle

or loose strands of silk with 2 wire bead threaders

Instructions

For this decorative knotting technique (Steps 1-5), refer to pages 70-71.

1 The first step is to make a loop with the silk – this will form the first half of the necklace closure. Fold the two lengths of thread in half to find the centre, keeping the needle ends on the right-hand side. (When you are making the square knots, the needle can be threaded through the loops of the knots.)

2 Pull up one of the loops thus formed so that this thread is about 6 cm shorter either side than the other.

3 Use the shorter thread, leaving a long tail of about 94 cm (37"), to bind about 2 cm (3/4") of the end loop of the longer thread with a button-hole stitch.

4 Join the two shorter threads in an overhand knot so that the closure loop is formed, leaving the two longer threads either side, ready to work the square knots.

5 Working with the two outer strands, make a series of square knots over the inner strands for a distance of about 6 cm (2") – or the correct measurement to fit your neck. The needle on the right-hand outer thread will help you to keep track of the pattern of knotting, as it is always the end with the needle which will pass through the knot loops.

6 Stiffen the ends of thread without needles with super glue. (When you need to pass a number of threads through a bead, you can use these stiffened ends first, followed by those on needles.)

7 Pass all the threads through an 8 mm goldstone bead. Make two square knots.

8 Separate the four strands into two – a left-hand outer and inner and a right-hand outer and inner. Make an overhand knot in each pair.

9 Follow the pattern of threading below, separating out and joining the threads together where necessary (see **Fig. b**).

2 glass tubes followed by 2 rocailles
3 pink glass beads followed by 2 goldstone beads
3 pink beads followed by 2 rocailles

10 Repeat the pattern until the last 2 glass tubes.
11 Make an overhand knot after each of the tubes, then join all threads together in two square knots.
12 Pass all the threads through a goldstone bead and then, keeping the needle ends to the right, use the two outer strands of thread to make the same length of square knots as you originally made at the beginning.
13 Finally, to make the closure you thread on the last goldstone bead and make an overhand knot close after it.
14 Seal the knot and when thoroughly dry, trim off the spare ends of thread.

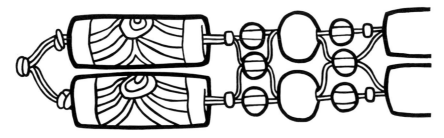

Fig. b

Gold Lacy Fringe

This project requires the off-loom weaving technique which is described in Techniques. The collar worn by the model opposit) is a two-pattern repeat collar; the instructions on page 72 are for a three-pattern repeat, so adjust them accordingly. The quantites of beads are sufficient to make a two- or three-pattern repeat collar measuring 36-40 cm (14-16"), including enough beads to make a clasp. It is always sensible to buy a few more as it is very frustrating to run out before you have finished the collar. Rocailles of any desired colour can be used – silver-lined or metallic finish rocailles are more sophisticated for evening wear. We have chosen a gold metallic finish: whichever type you use, check first that the finish is reasonably permanent.

Necklace

Materials

25 gms size 11/0 gold-finish rocailles

5 gms size 8/0 gold-finish rocailles

2 gold-coloured calottes

Gold-plated clasp

3-4 m approx. fine strong thread

Beading needle (size 10)

Instructions

The collar is made by following the line drawings and instructions on page 72. The size 8/0 beads are used where the shaded beads are indicated and at the bottom to form the clover leaf pattern. The necklace can be finished either with a clasp and calottes or a loop and bead closure (see page 70).

Moghul Necklace and Earrings

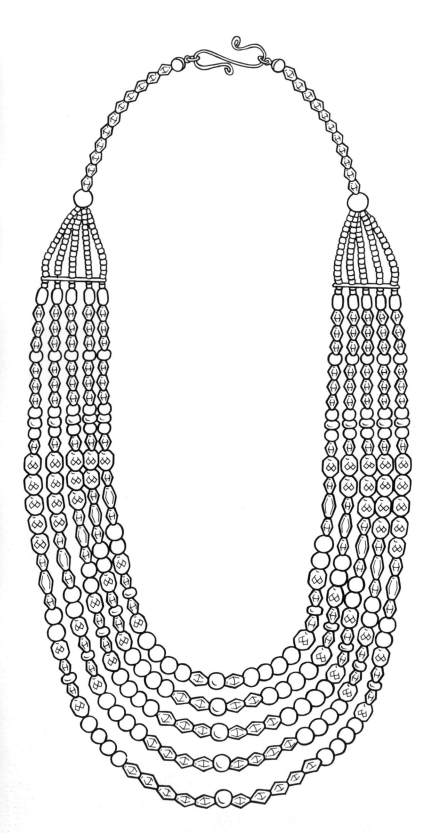

This necklace is made with glass beads – sapphire blue, 'moonstone' and rainbow-coated and plastic beads – deep blue 'miracle'. Different types of the same size and colour of beads have been used for a varied textural effect. However, this is not essential – if you prefer, the 8 mm clear beads can be all faceted rainbow, or all round rainbow – just remember to adapt the quantities accordingly. Any toning colours may be used but transparent or translucent colours look best. The necklace should be strung on a double strand of fine, strong thread. A necklace design board is useful for laying the beads out in order. However, if you do not have one, use a folded cloth to make a groove. You will need glue, snipe-nosed pliers and scissors for this project.

Fig. a

Necklace

Materials

10 x 4 x 6 mm blue oval glass beads

7 x 8 mm blue 'miracle' beads (two of these should have fairly large holes as they take multiple strands of threads)

20 x 6 mm blue 'miracle' beads

50 x 8 mm blue diamond-shaped beads

112 x 5 mm blue diamond-shaped beads

50 x 8 mm faceted rainbow-coated crystal beads

60 x 8 mm clear, round rainbow-coated beads

10 x 10 mm clear diamond-shaped beads

30 x 6 mm 'moonstone' glass beads

Size 8/0 silver-lined, rainbow-coated blue rocailles (152 taken from 18 gm pack)

2 x 5-holed, silver-plated spacer bars

2 x silver-plated calottes

2 x silver-plated, oval jump rings

1 x silver-plated, snake clasp

5 m approx. silk or polyester thread in toning colour, used doubled

1 wire bead threader

Instructions

The lower part of the necklace consists of five graded strings (the smaller beads at the top, increasing in size towards the bottom). These should be threaded up first – the pattern of threading is straightforward if you follow **Fig. a** carefully. Save 2 x 8 mm blue 'miracle' beads and 22 x 5 mm blue diamond-shaped beads for the upper single strands of the necklace.

1 Lay out the beads for the first string, following **Fig. a**.
2 Use a double strand of thread on a wire needle.
3 Allowing about 20 cm thread spare at the beginning of the strand, make a slip knot.

4 Thread on 2 rocailles, followed by the rest of the beads in the correct order.

5 Finish with 2 rocailles, pull the thread taut, make a slip knot, leaving about 20 cm spare thread after it.

6 String the other four strands in the same way.

7 When all five rows are complete, arrange them in order from the shortest to the longest.

8 Undo the first slip knot of the shortest string, and pass the wire needle onto the thread.

9 Take a five-holed spacer bar and pass the needle through the first hole.

10 Thread on 14 rocailles after the spacer, remove the needle and make a slip knot in the thread.

11 Using the second spacer bar, repeat this process at the other end.

12 Do the same with the other four strings, making sure to keep them in order, until all five are attached to the spacer bars. (NB The 2nd strand has 13 rocailles, the 3rd has 12, the 4th has 13, the 5th has 14.)

13 Undo all the slip knots on one side of the necklace, straighten out the ends of thread and pulling all of them taut, make an overhand knot close to the rocailles. Seal with glue.

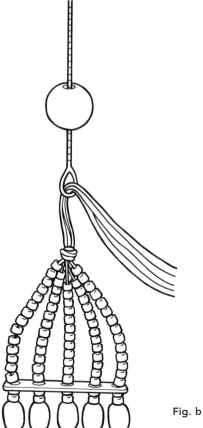

Fig. b

14 Take one of the reserved 8 mm blue beads and thread all these ends through using a wire threader* (see **Fig. b**).

15 Push the 8 mm bead down the thread and make a knot after it, keeping the thread taut.

16 String on 11 of the reserved 5 mm blue beads, make an overhand knot close to the beads and seal it.

17 Fix a calotte over the knot and trim away the spare ends.

18 Repeat the process for the other end of the necklace.

19 Finish with jump rings linking the calottes to the snake clasp.

Fig. c

* When you reach the upper part of the necklace, if you cannot get all the threads through the 8 mm beads, use this alternative method (see **Fig. c**):

  1 Check the knot after the rocailles to see that it is firm and sealed.

  2 Pass as many threads as you can through the 8 mm bead.

  3 Trim away the unused threads close to the knot.
     Return to Step 15 to complete the necklace.

Earrings

Materials

26 x 5 mm blue diamond-shaped beads

18 x 6 mm faceted rainbow crystal beads

12 x 6 mm 'moonstone' beads

58 x size 11/0 blue silver-lined rainbow rocailles (taken from small pack)

2 x 3-holed silver-plated spacer-bars

2 small silver-plated calottes

1 pair of silver-plated earfittings

2 m approx. fine polyester, used doubled

1 wire bead threader

Instructions

Divide the beads into two piles, one for each earring. Each earring has three strands, all threaded in the same way, except the centre strand has one extra blue bead and one extra rocaille below the spacer bar, and one less rocaille above the bar. Follow **Fig. d** for the pattern of threading.

1 As each strand is completed, make a temporary slip knot until all are finished.
2 Undo all slip knots, and gather the strands together to knot closely to the rocailles.
3 Seal with glue, fix a calotte over the knot and trim away the spare threads.
4 Hang the calotte from an earfitting (see **Fig. e**).
5 The second earring is completed in the same way.

Fig. d   Fig. e

Amber Horn Collar and Earrings

This necklace is made with horn beads, stained an amber colour, gold-plated plastic and copper-coloured metal beads. The golden drops hanging from the base give added interest, but for a simpler look these may be omitted. The necklace looks best if it sits just at the base of the throat, so if necessary, adjust the length. Adding more small copper beads will make it longer, or if you need it shorter, remove a long bead from either side (if necessary substituting some small copper beads). You will need glue for knots, snipe-nosed pliers, scissors and wire cutters for this project.

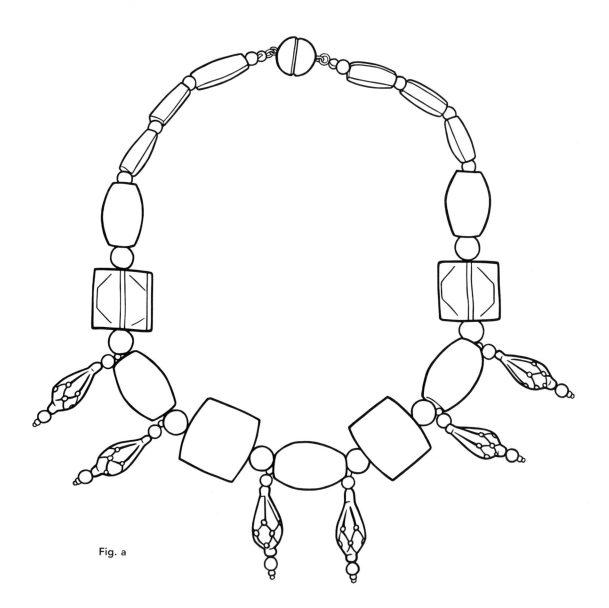

Fig. a

Necklace

Materials

5 oval golden-amber horn beads

2 bevelled reddish-amber horn beads

2 flat faceted, reddish-amber horn beads

6 long reddish-amber horn beads

8 x 8 mm copper beads

20 x 5 mm copper beads

12 x 2.5 mm gold-plated beads

6 gold-plated plastic 'Tuscan' drops

6 gold-plated headpins

Gold-plated clasp

2 gold-plated calottes

1 m approx. medium-weight polyester thread, used doubled

Needle/wire bead threader

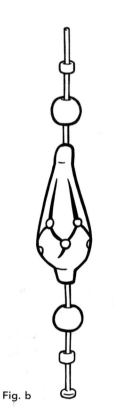

Fig. b

Instructions

The first step is to make six drop components (eight if you are making the matching earrings).

1 Thread an eyepin with the following bead pattern (see **Fig. b**):
   1 x 2.5 mm gold-plated bead
   1 x 5 mm copper bead
   1 drop
   1 x 5 mm copper bead
   1 x 2.5 mm gold-plated bead
2 Allowing about 8 mm (1/4") of spare wire after the last bead, cut the headpin. Do not discard the waste wire.

3 Using round-nosed pliers, make a loop after the last bead and close it firmly.

4 Using the waste wire from the first headpin as a measure, cut the remaining five headpins to the correct length.

5 Make the other five components in the same way as the first.

6 Thread the needle and make a slip knot at the end of the double strand.

7 Thread on the beads according to **Fig. a**.

8 Try the necklace for length and adjust if necessary.

9 Knot the end threads, seal with a little glue and fix on the calottes.

10 Attach the necklace clasp.

Earrings

Materials

2 gold-plated plastic 'Tuscan' drops

4 x 5 mm copper beads

4 x 2.5 mm gold-plated beads

2 gold-plated headpins

1 pair gold-plated earfittings with loop

Instructions

1 Make two drop components as described in necklace instructions.

2 Attach to earfittings using pliers and make sure to close the loops firmly.

Twisted Green and Purple Strands and Earrings

This necklace is made up of four knotted strands, twisted and linked together with a large, hinged ring. You can use two toning colours as we have done here, one single colour or strands of different colours for a multi-coloured effect. You need glue, scissors and snipe-nosed pliers. The following quantities are for both the necklace and earrings. Put aside 48 green beads and 2 purple beads for the earrings.

Necklace

Materials

3 x 30 gms 5 mm green frosted beads

3 x 30 gms 5 mm purple frosted beads

7 m approx. medium thickness strong thread

or 14 m approx. fine strong thread used doubled

1 pair earclips with 15 mm pierced disc fronts

Necklace shortener clasp

Wire bead threader

Instructions

1 Starting and finishing each strand with a slip knot, thread up two strands of purple and two of green beads to measure approximately 1 m each.
2 Make sure all strands are of the same length. Take the first strand and pull taut both ends of the thread until the beads are drawn together.
3 Finish off the strands by making a reef (square) knot. Seal the knot with glue and when dry, trim away the spare ends and move the beads together to cover it.
4 Repeat this process for the other three strands.
5 Take all four strands and hook a finger into the loop formed at either end.
6 Give the strands a number of twists then link the end loops with the clasp.

Earrings

Instructions

1 Secure the thread at the centre of the disc. String on the centre bead and secure.
2 Bring thread to the front of the disc and pass on sufficient beads to lie closely in a circle around the centre bead. Secure at the back. Cover the surface of the bead.
3 Clip the disc onto an earring back by squeezing the metal lugs over it.
4 Repeat for other earring. (See Techniques, page 82 for illustrations.)

Safety Pin Necklace and Earrings

Safety pins threaded with beads and then strung together create stunning jewellery. When strung through the coil of the pin, as the bottoms are fatter than the tops, the string will lie in a curve. In order to make the curve more gradual, space the pins with a bead. For this project you will require scissors, glue and snipe-nosed pliers. If you are making your own clasp and earring loops, you will also need wire cutters and round-nosed pliers (see Techniques, pages 80-81).

Fig. a

Necklace

Materials

72 x silver-coloured safety pins (2.5 cm/1")

73 x 3 mm silver-plated metal beads

72 x 5 mm red glass diamond-shaped beads

5 gms size 8/0 rainbow-coated, silver-lined red rocailles

5 gms size 11/0 silver-lined orange rocailles

2 silver-plated calottes

4 silver-plated leather calottes

Silver-plated snake clasp

2 silver-plated jump rings

1/2 m leather/thick cord thonging

3/4 m medium thickness thread used doubled

Wire bead threader

Instructions

1 Thread the pins with beads.

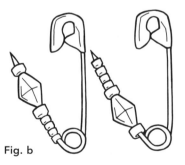

Fig. b

2 String the pins together through the end coils, spacing them out with a silver bead.

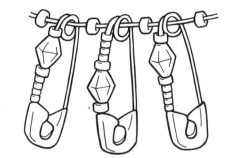

Fig. c

3 Draw them together.

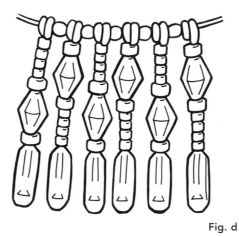

Fig. d

4 Finish with a knot and calotte either side.

5 Cut leather thonging into two lengths and fix a leather calotte on one end of each.

6 Hook the calotte loops of the threaded pins into the leather calottes.

7 Try the necklace around your neck and cut the lengths of thong shorter if necessary.

8 Finish the ends with the remaining two leather calottes. Attach these to the snake clasp by means of the jump rings.

Earrings

Materials

22 silver-coloured safety pins (2.5 cm/1")

24 x 3 mm silver-plated metal beads

22 x 5 mm red glass diamond-shaped beads

Rocailles taken from 5 gms packs used for necklace

2 x silver-plated earfittings with hooks

2 x ready-made teardrop loops

Instructions

1 Separate the bead quantities into two heaps.

2 Thread the 11 safety pins with beads as before.

3 String onto fine teardrop loop, alternating with silver beads.

4 Attach to earfitting

5 Repeat for the other earring.

Cascade Necklace and Earrings

The lacy look of this collar and bib necklace and earrings is achieved by the use of diamond-shaped, open-work spacers. This particular necklace is made with black rainbow-coated, faceted beads and silver-coloured fittings – it would look just as effective with crystal-coloured beads and gold-coloured fittings. If you use spacers other than the ones used here, ensure that the holes run from side to side and not front to back.

The ends of the first three rows which form the collar may be finished with calottes. The ends which form the bib must be finished with gimp. It is essential to have mastered this technique before attempting to make this necklace (use **method b** on page 61). If you prefer to use gimp for all end finishings, you will need six extra pieces instead of the calotttes. The tools you will need for both the necklace and earrings are snipe-nosed and round-nosed pliers, wire cutters, scissors and glue for sealing knots.

Necklace

Materials

76 x 8 mm black, faceted glass beads, plain or rainbow-coated

5 gms size 8/0 black or rainbow-coated rocailles

15 x 11/0 rocailles

3 x 11/0 rocailles (for securing knots if using clamshell calottes)

31 x diamond-shaped spacers (hole running from side to side)

1 x wire triangle link

1 x 15 x 9 mm black, faceted glass drop, plain or rainbow-coated

2 x 3-ringed necklace ends/spacer hangers

10 x 4 x 6mm oval jump rings

6 calottes (preferably clamshell)

6 x 6 mm lengths of gimp

3 silver-coloured eyepins

1 silver-coloured headpin

1 silver-coloured hook for closure

5 m approx. fine, strong black thread, used doubled

Wire bead threader

Instructions

It is helpful to count out the number of large faceted beads and the number of diamond spacers required for each row of the necklace:

Row 1	20 faceted beads	10 spacers
Row 2	20 faceted beads	11 spacers
Row 3	20 faceted beads	4 spacers
Row 4	6 faceted beads	3 spacers
Row 5	4 faceted beads	2 spacers
Row 6	2 faceted beads	1 spacer

Begin with the triple row collar:

1 Using a double strand of thread, knot the end and hide with a calotte.

2 Follow the pattern of threading as in **Fig. a**:

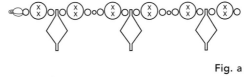

1 large rocaille
1 faceted bead
1 large rocaille
1 spacer
1 large rocaille
1 faceted bead
1 large rocaille
1 small rocaille

Fig. a

This pattern is repeated until you have 10 spacers threaded in this way. Finish the row with a calotte and lay the row down so that all the spacers hang downwards.

3 For the second row (see **Fig. b**), start again with a calotte and then thread on:

1 large rocaille
1 new spacer
1 large rocaille
1 faceted bead
1 large rocaille
first spacer from the row above
1 large rocaille
1 faceted bead

Fig. b

This sequence is repeated until all the spacers from the row above have been picked up, and the row is finished with 1 large rocaille, a new spacer and 1 large rocaille. You should now have 11 spacers hanging down from Row 2. Finish with a calotte.

4 For the third row (see **Fig. c**), start again with a calotte and then thread on:

1 large rocaille
first spacer from Row 2
1 large rocaille
1 faceted bead
1 large rocaille
1 small rocaille
1 large rocaille
1 faceted bead
1 large rocaille
second spacer from Row 2

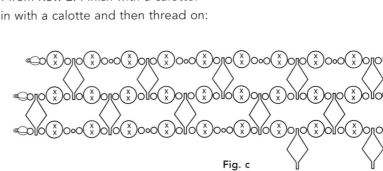

Fig. c

Repeat this sequence until 4 spacers have been picked up from Row 2.

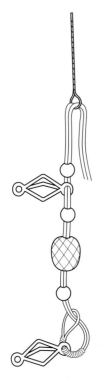

Fig. d

5 Continue to use the same pattern of threading but replace the small rocaille each time with a new spacer until you have 4 new spacers hanging down from this row. These will lie in the centre of the row. The remaining half of the row is completed in reverse order to the first and finished with a calotte.

6 The remaining, decreasing rows are finished with gimp ends which protect the thread curled around the rings of the first and last spacers hanging from the row above (see **Fig. d**). Follow **Fig. e** for the order of threading. Note that the last spacer suspended in the centre is hung with a triangular link whose two ends are squeezed into the horizontal hole of the drop.

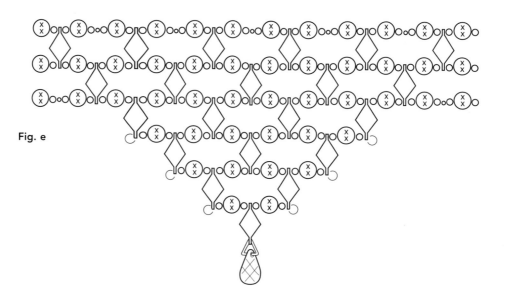

Fig. e

7 To finish off the necklace with an adjustable closure, link both the three-ring necklace ends to the three calottes by means of the jump rings.

8 Thread a headpin with an 8 mm faceted bead and cut the wire, allowing 8 mm protruding after the bead. Make a neat loop in the wire, using round-nosed pliers.

9 Set aside for the moment.

10 Thread each of the remaining 3 faceted beads onto the eyepins and complete in the same way.

11 Link one of the eyepin components to the ring of one of the necklace ends using an oval jump ring and attach the hook to the other loop of the eyepin (see **Fig. f**).

12 Use the remaining three jump rings to link together the headpin component and the two eyepin components and attach them to the ring of the other necklace end (see **Fig. g**).

13 The necklace is closed by hooking into one of the jump rings at the other end.

Fig. f

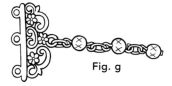

Fig. g

Earrings

Materials

8 x 8 mm black faceted beads, plain or rainbow-coated

6 x 15 x 9 mm black faceted drops, plain or rainbow-coated

(pierced horizontally at the apex)

8 x size 8/0 rocailles

2 x 3-ringed hangers

4 x 4 x 6 mm oval jump rings

8 x silver-coloured diamond-shaped spacers

8 x silver-coloured eyepins

6 x silver-coloured wire triangles

1 pair earfittings with hooks

Instructions

1 Take one eyepin and thread on a faceted bead. Allowing 8 mm spare for a loop, cut to the appropriate length.

2 Remove the bead and use this eyepin as a measure to cut 3 more.

3 Thread a bead onto each eyepin and shape the loops at the spare end but do not close them up.

4 Take an eyepin and thread it with 1 rocaille, 1 faceted bead and 1 rocaille.

5 Allowing 8 mm spare to form a loop, cut to the appropriate length.

6 Remove the beads and use the eyepin as a measure to cut the remaining three eyepins.

7 Thread each eyepin as before and shape the spare wire into a loop.

8 Assemble the eyepin components in the manner shown in **Fig. h**, closing up all loops as you go, and finishing each dangle with a triangle and drop.

Fig. h

Tasselled Red and Black Necklace and Earrings

This necklace is made using a dramatic contrast of opaque red and glass beads teamed with antique finish, silver-plated plastic beads. If you prefer a different colourway, transparent toning colours will give a more subtle effect and gold instead of silver beads will give a warmer look to the necklace. Whether you use gold or silver beads, please make sure that the holes are large enough to take five strands of thread. The silver beads used for the earrings (which match the central necklace pendant) are very light in weight so do not drag on the earlobes. For the necklace, you will need glue, scissors and snipe-nosed pliers and for the earrings, wire cutters and round-nosed pliers.

Fig. a

Necklace

Materials

1 x 10 mm black glass bead (shaded on **Figs. b & c**)

34 x 8 mm black glass beads (shaded on **Figs. b & c**)

122 x 6 mm black glass beads (shaded on **Figs. b & c**)

251 x 6 mm red glass beads

1 large silver-plated plastic bead

(large hole running from top to bottom)

4 x 20 mm silver-plated plastic beads (large-holed)

11 x 12 mm silver-plated plastic discs (large-holed)

1 round silver-plated plastic clasp

2 silver-plated calottes

8 m medium thickness black polyester

Instructions

The threading of this necklace begins at the centre tassel and is worked up each side. Before you begin, put aside these beads for the tassel – 10 mm black bead, 4 x 8 mm black beads, 8 x 6 mm black beads and 11 x 6 mm red beads. Divide the rest of the beads into two equal amounts per colour, one for each side of the necklace.

1 Cut the thread into five separate lengths of 1.5 m
2 Coat about 3 cm of both ends of each thread with a thin layer of glue or nail polish and allow to dry.
3 Thread the centre strand with the 10 mm black bead, and move it down the thread until it is positioned half-way.
4 Pass both stiffened ends of thread through 1 x 6 mm black bead, 3 x 6 mm red, 1 x 6 mm black.
5 The other 4 tassel strands are threaded in a similar way, but each strand starts with an 8 mm black bead, and in the first two of these, 1 red bead is omitted and in the second two strands, the bottom 6 mm black and 1 red bead are omitted (see **Fig. b** which shows the beads separated out to demonstrate the pattern of threading).

Fig. b

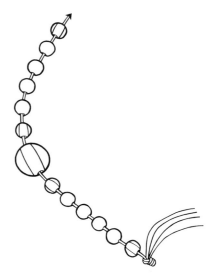

6   Gather all the threads together, pass them through the long silver pendant bead and make a knot close after it.

7   Pass a 12 mm silver disc over this knot, separate the 10 strands into two lots of five and knot these close after the bead (see **Fig. b**).

8   Starting on the left-hand side of the necklace, thread four of the strands (leaving the centre one for the moment) in the following manner (see **Fig. c**):
    1 small black bead; 4 small red; 1 small black; 1 large black;
    1 small black; 4 small red; 1 small black

9   Thread the centre strand in the same way but OMIT the first small black bead.

10 Gather all five threads and pull taut, so that all the beads are forced together, pass them through a silver disc and make a knot close after it.

11 Thread on a large silver bead.

12 Make a knot after the large bead, and slip a small silver disc over it.

13 Using the necklace illustration as a guide (**Fig. a**), thread the rest of the beads in the same way (Steps 8-9) until the left hand side is completed.

14 Finish with an overhand knot after the last silver disc, apply a little glue, then fix a calotte over the knot.

15 Complete the right-hand side of the necklace in the same way; trim away the excess thread and attach each calotte to the necklace clasp.

Fig. c

Earrings

Materials

2 x long silver-plated, plastic pendant beads (hole running from top to bottom)

2 x 8 mm black glass beads (shaded on **Fig. d**)

2 x 6 mm red glass beads

2 silver-plated headpins

1 pair silver-plated earhooks

Instructions

1   Thread each headpin with 1 black bead, 1 silver bead, 1 red bead (see **Fig. d**).

2   Cut the pins, leaving approx 8 mm spare wire after the red bead.

3   Bend this end into a loop using round-nosed pliers.

4   Hang the pin from an earfitting.

5   Complete the second earring in the same way.

Fig. d

Multi-Strand Necklace of Carnelian Chips and Earrings

The carnelian chips are interspersed at random with other semi-precious beads and silver beads in various sizes. If desired, glass beads may be substituted for the jasper and turquoise beads; silver-plated beads for the silver beads. If you would like the necklace shorter at the front, make each of the lower strands shorter than the given lengths; the same applies to the earrings but do not shorten by more than 2.5 cm (1") as they will look unbalanced. The tools you will need for the necklace are glue, scissors and snipe-nosed pliers; for the earrings you will also need round-nosed pliers and wire cutters.

Fig. a

Pewter Necklace and Earrings

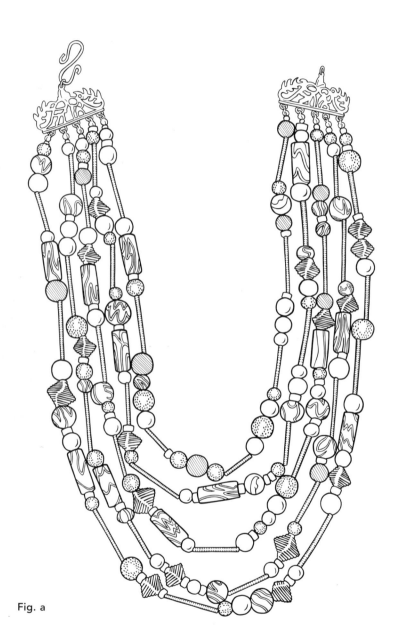

Fig. a

This five-strand necklace uses a variety of beads in silvery, grey tones – lac, 'crackle', 'karak' and 'miracle' – and assorted wire beads in a silver finish. It is threaded in a random manner, so that the heaviness is broken up and lightened by the fine, long silver-coiled tubes. Before you actually start threading, make sure that the strands lie comfortably in graduated curves. I often have a dry run-through and string the beads on nylon monofilament. Two sizes of silver coil beads have been used; the lengths of these tend to vary but they can be shortened with wire cutters. The handmade lac beads also vary in size so it is useful to have a few spare rondels to adjust the balance if necessary. It is not essential to use all the types or various sizes of the beads here – substituting the plastic beads with hollow metal beads may be more economical. For the necklace, you will need glue, scissors and snipe-nosed pliers. If you are making the earrings, you will also need round-nosed pliers and wire cutters.

Necklace

Materials

12 lac cylinders

13 x 10-12 mm lac beads (grey-white marbled)

7 x 6-8 mm lac beads (grey-white marbled)

15 x 8 mm plastic miracle beads (silver grey)

17 x 6 mm plastic miracle beads (silver grey)

7 x 10 mm plastic crackle beads (matt, textured pewter finish)

10 x 6 mm plastic crackle beads (matt, textured pewter finish)

6 x 8 mm crackle beads (matt, textured silver finish)

11 x 6 mm crackle beads (matt, textured silver finish)

3 x 10 mm karak beads (shiny, pewter finish)

6 x 8 mm karak beads (shiny, pewter finish)

3 x 10 mm karak beads (shiny, silver finish)

9 x 8 mm karak beads (shiny, silver finish)

22 x short silver coil tubes (15 mm)

16 x long silver coil tubes (20 mm)

3 x 12 mm wire diamond-shaped beads

13 x 10 mm wire diamond-shaped beads

38 x 6 mm rondels (silver finish)

10 x 2.5 mm silver-plated beads

10 calottes (silver finish)

2 x 5-ringed necklace ends (silver finish)

2 oval jump rings (silver finish)

1 snake clasp (silver finish)

5 m approx. strong toning thread used doubled

Wire bead threader

Instructions

The rows of beads measure as follows: Row 1: 34 cm (13 1/2"); Row 2: 38 cm (15"); Row 3: 41 cm (16"); Row 4: 45 cm (17 3/4"); Row 5: 48 cm (19")

1 Lay the beads out randomly in rows to measure as above. Try to avoid using too many similar beads together as they cause the necklace to bunch-up. Set aside the tiny, 2.5 mm silver beads.

2 Using the necklace diagram (**Fig. a**) as a rough guide, thread each row of beads on a length of monofilament, starting with the shortest. Lay each row in a curve to follow the preceding one. You will be able to see if the necklace looks balanced – adjust the beads accordingly.

3 When you are happy with the design of the necklace, make a knot at the beginning of the strong toning thread and begin threading 'for real', starting and finishing with a 2.5 mm silver bead from the ones set aside.

4 Fix a calotte over each finishing knot and attach each row in sequence to the necklace ends.

5 Make the closure by linking the snake clasp to the necklace ends with jump rings.

Earrings

Materials

2 x 12 mm diamond-shaped wire beads

2 x 10 mm diamond-shaped wire beads

2 x 10 mm plastic karak beads (shiny, silver finish)

2 x 10 mm plastic karak beads (shiny, pewter finish)

2 x 8 mm plastic karak beads (shiny, silver finish)

4 x 8 mm plastic karak beads (shiny, pewter finish)

2 x 6-8 mm lac beads (grey-white marbled)

2 x 18 mm lac tubes (grey-white marbled)

2 x long wire coil tubes (approx. 25 mm)

4 x short wire coil tubes (approx. 20 mm)

4 headpins (75 mm)

2 headpins (50 mm)

(If you are making your own pins from wire, finish the bottoms with loops)

2 x 3-holed, silver-plated spacer-hangers

1 pair fittings (silver finish)

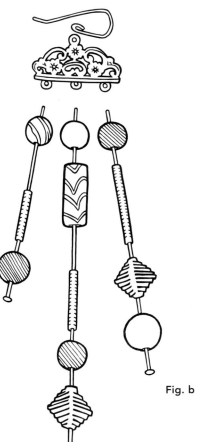

Fig. b

Instructions

1 Thread the headpins according to **Fig. b**.

2 Cut the pins to the appropriate lengths, leaving approx. 8 mm spare wire to bend into loops which will hang from the rings of the spacers.

3 Reverse the positions of the two outer pins for the second earring.

4 Hang the assembled earrings from the loops of the earfittings.

Cinnabar and Cloisonné Necklace and Earrings

This necklace is made with carved red 'cinnabar' beads, teamed with red cloisonné beads, threaded and knotted at intervals on heavy silk of a toning colour. The cinnabar beads could be substituted by any carved wooden bead e.g. ebony with black cloisonné. This necklace does not require a clasp as the finishing knot is hidden inside the tassel. For the necklace you will need glue and scissors and for the earrings, wire cutters and round-nosed pliers.

Fig. a

Necklace

Materials

18 x 12 mm carved cinnabar, laquered beads

5 x 12 mm red cloisonné beads

1 x 14 mm carved cinnabar bead

1 x square cinnabar bead (hole running from top to bottom)

2 x 2 m cards of heavy braided silk with attached needle

or multiple strands of finer silk used doubled with wire bead threaders

Instructions

Four thicknesses of thread must pass through the 2 bottom beads and two thicknesses through the others, so check first. The necklace is made with two strands each with its own needle or wire threader, starting at the centre front. Both needles pass through all the beads.

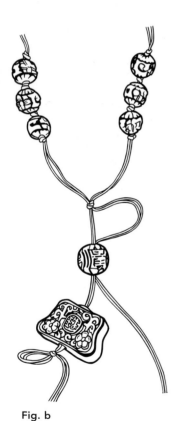

1 Join the ends of the threads in a slip knot, leaving a tail of approx. 5 cm (2") and thread on the square cinnabar bead followed by the large round one.
2 Make an overhand knot 19 cm (7 1/2") further up the thread from the round cinnabar bead.
3 Thread on the first group of three cinnabar beads, making a knot before and after each one.
4 The remaining beads are threaded at intervals of 2.5 cm (1"): 1 cloisonné bead and a group of 3 cinnabar beads, each bead knotted before and after. This pattern is repeated five times (see **Fig. a**).
5 When the last group of three cinnabar beads has been threaded, bring the thread down so that they are on the same level as the first three. About 4 cm (1 1/2") below the beads, knot all the threads together, passing the square cinnabar bead and the large round one through the loop of the knot.
6 Pass the new threads through the large round bead (see **Fig. b**).
7 Push the bead up the thread and knot close after it.
8 Undo the slip knot below the square bead, pass the new threads through it and knot closely after the bead. Do not cut the threads yet.

Fig. b

Tassel

Materials

10 m fine silk

Matchbox as a base for binding the silk

50 cm approx. silk threaded on a needle

Short length of fine wire (fuse wire will do)

Instructions

1 Bind the thread firmly and evenly around a matchbox lengthwise.
2 Slide the piece of wire under the threads at one end and twist into a loose loop.
3 At the other end, cut through the threads cleanly.
4 Carefully slide the loop of wire up the threads and twist it to hold them in place.
5 Now you are ready to attach the tassel to the necklace. Take the threads at the bottom of the square bead and knot them tightly around the middle of the tassel threads using a square (reef) knot (see **Fig. c**).
6 Remove the twist of wire. Smooth the tassel threads down over the knot and holding the ends, complete the tassel by binding tightly with the spare silk so that the necklace knot is hidden beneath (see **Fig. a**).
7 Trim both tassel and necklace threads.

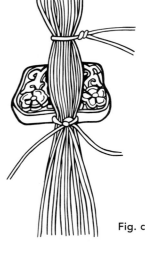

Fig. c

Earrings

Materials

2 x 12 mm carved cinnabar beads

2 x 10 mm red cloisonné beads

6 x 3 mm gold-plated metal beads

4 x 8 mm gold-plated bead caps

2 gold-plated headpins

1 pair gold-coloured earfittings

Instructions

1 Thread the beads on the headpin as shown in **Fig. d**.
2 Cut the pin to the correct length, leaving about 8 mm spare wire to make a loop.
3 Hang the pin from an earring hook.
4 Make the second earring in the same way.

Fig. d

Peacock Bead Fringe and Earrings

The design of this project is inspired by a traditional Comanche weave pattern shown in Therese Spears' *Beaded Earrings*. Both these pieces of jewellery are made with embroidery beads – size 11/0 rocailles and size 3''' bugles. Rocailles with a sparkle – silver-lined, transparent, iridescent or metallic finishes – are prettiest for evening wear but they do not have such a long life expectancy as non-coated beads. Take care when using metallic beads as the finish on cheaper ones tends to wear off when worn against the skin.

It is best to allow more beads than strictly necessary as any misshapen or oddly sized beads will be discarded. Allow plenty of fine, strong thread in a toning colour – bonded nylon is excellent as it resists tangling, otherwise rub thread over some beeswax or a candle. The thread has to pass a number of times through the beads, so your needle should be fine. I used a split, big eye needle for this project, though you can use a fine, size 10 beading needle. For both the necklace and earrings, you will need scissors and glue.

If you have never done this type of bead weaving start with the earrings to get into practice for the longer piece. The project is worked from left to right; if you are left-handed, reverse the instructions.

When designing your own necklace from scratch, it is best to work out the pattern on paper. Make a rough drawing and then use graph paper to plan the detail. For repeating reversed patterns it is only necessary to draw up half the pattern – the method of working is reversed for the other half and then repeated as many times as required. It is very important to count correctly as you work: a missed bead or one too many will ruin the pattern.

Earrings

Materials

4 gms iridescent green/purple rocailles, size 11/0 (iris)

4 gms iridescent green/purple bugles, size 3''

2 gms silver-lined rainbow green rocailles, size 11/0 (green)

2 gms gold metallic (or silver-lined) rocailles, size 11/0 (gold)

1 pair gold-coloured earfittings

5 m approx. fine, strong black thread, used single

Beeswax/candle

Split 'big eye' beading needle

or 1-2 fine beading needles (size 10)

Colour Key

 Iridescent green/purple (iris)

⊗ Silver-lined rainbow green (green)

◯ Gold metallic (gold)

Instructions

Add on extra thread by means of a reef knot, and conceal ends in adjacent beads so that the knot is hidden in the main body of the work.

1 Thread a beading needle on each end of a 4 m length of thread. (If using only 1 needle, pass the end without the needle through the bead first).
2 Thread on 2 bugle beads and position them about 1 m down the thread.
3 Pass the right hand thread through the first bugle as shown in **Fig. a**.
4 Pull both ends of thread until the bugles are drawn together to lie parallel (see **Fig. b-c**)

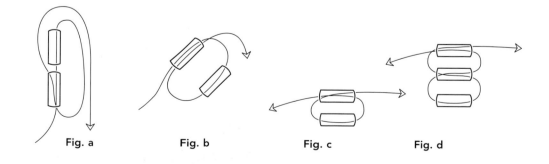

Fig. a   Fig. b   Fig. c   Fig. d

5 Pass both ends of thread in opposite directions through a third bugle and pull gently so that the bugles line up but lie flat (see **Fig. d**).

6 Add another 8 bugles keeping an even tension so that they lie flat but close to each other (**Fig. e**).

7 The upper part of the earring is completed first, using the shorter end of the thread. The rows of beads decrease by one to form a triangle as you move upwards. Start with one row of gold beads which are positioned above the bugles. Hold the bugles and the long tail of thread firmly together at the end so they do not separate.

8 Pick up 1 gold bead on the short thread and pass the needle under the loop of thread, between the first and second bugle at the top of the row (see **Fig. f**).

9 Pass the needle and thread back through the bead in the direction shown in **Fig. g**. Pull the thread taut until the bead turns to lie flat on the top of the bugles and repeat with the second gold bead (see **Fig. h**).

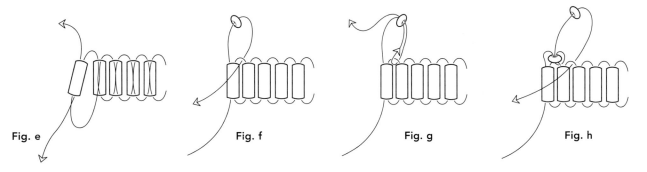

Fig. e   Fig. f   Fig. g   Fig. h

10 Continue to do this until you have 10 gold beads sitting firmly above the bugles then turn the work around and begin the second row in the same way as the first, using green beads (see **Fig. i**).

11 Follow **Fig. j** for the pattern of threading. You drop a bead on each row until the last row which has 2 green beads, thus forming a triangular shape.

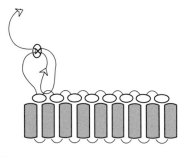

Fig. i

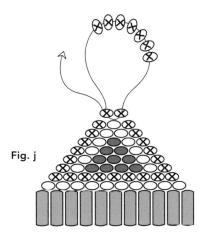

Fig. j

12 Pick up 8 green beads on the thread and take the needle down though the first bead at the apex of the triangle and up through the second, pulling the thread taut so that the beads curl into a loop (**Fig. j**).

13 Repeat this a second time to give added strength, then make a double knot over the thread at the bottom of the loop of beads.

14 If you can get the tail of this through the beads a third time to hide the end, do so; if not, seal knot with glue and trim closely.

15 The bottom of the earring is beaded using the long tail of thread. Pass on to the thread the following sequence of beads (**Fig. k**):

1 gold
1 green
1 iris
1 gold
1 green
11 iris
1 green
1 gold
1 bugle
1 gold
1 green

16 Form the clover leaf shape at the bottom by threading on 3 gold beads. You then take the thread back through the last green bead, up the strand, and through the bugle at the top, pulling the thread so that the beads lie together, but not too taut.

17 Bring the thread down through the next bugle bead to bead the second string.

18 Each successive string is increased by 1 iris bead after the first green bead, until you reach the middle string which has 5 extra iris beads (the pattern will quickly become clear).

19 After the middle string (string 6) begin to decrease again by 1 iris bead.

20 Finish by knotting around the thread after the last bugle bead. As before, try to conceal the tail end of thread inside the beads, otherwise seal with glue and trim.

21 Complete the second earring in the same way and attach both to a pair of earfittings.

Fig. k

Necklace

Materials

18 gms iridescent green/purple rocailles, size 11/0 (iris)

14 gms iridescent green/purple bugles, size 3''''

8 gms silver-lined rainbow green rocailles, size 11/0 (green)

16 gms gold metallic (or silver-lined) rocailles, size 11/0 (gold)

1 x 6 mm gold metallic bead

15 m approx. fine, strong black beading thread, used single

Beeswax/candle

Split 'big eye' beading needle

or 2 fine beading needles (size 10)

Instructions

The fringe is hung centrally from a collar formed by 135 bugle beads, which are threaded in the same way as those in the earrings. Work with an even tension so that the beads lie flat but close to each other.

1 Start with a length of thread 6 m long and position the first bugle about half way down the thread.
2 Follow **Figs. a-e** to thread up 80 bugles, leaving the tails of thread protruding.
3 Go back to the first bugle and pass a fresh 6 m length of thread through it. Balance the amount of thread either side, and add the remaining 55 bugles in the same way as before (see **Fig. e**).
4 When the last bugle has been threaded, the first half of the adjustable necklace closure is formed by beading the two ends of thread with gold rocailles (see **Fig. l**). When the last loop is completed, the threads are taken back through the opposite rows of beads, the upper thread is brought down through the first bugle and left for the moment and the lower thread is taken up through the bugle and a gold rocaille is threaded (see **Fig. m**).

Fig. l

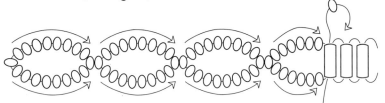

Fig. m

5 The row of bugles is topped by a row of gold rocailles in the same way as the earrings. Thread on the gold rocailles following **Figs. f-h** until you reach the last bugle.

6 Remove the needle from the thread and leave this end for the moment. Turn the work over so that the lower edge is now uppermost, and pass the needle onto the tail of thread left over from the first half of the necklace closure. Bead along this edge as before until 40 rocailles have been secured in position and then turn the work over again to start the fringe.

7 Bring the thread down through bugle 41 and thread on the following beads:
1 gold rocaille, 1 green, 1 bugle, 1 green, 3 iris, 1 gold, 1 bugle, 4 gold

8 The thread is then taken back through the beads to form a clover leaf pattern at the end (see **Fig. n**).

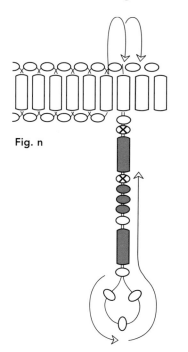

Fig. n

9 Bring the thread down through the next bugle to start the second string of the fringe.

10 Follow **Fig. o** for the colour sequence of each string. Once you have completed a few strings the pattern will quickly emerge, but do remember to count the beads carefully. Each string is increased each time by one bead until you reach the 28th string which has 21 iris beads in the centre of the triangle. After this the strings are decreased by one bead, following the pattern in reverse order.

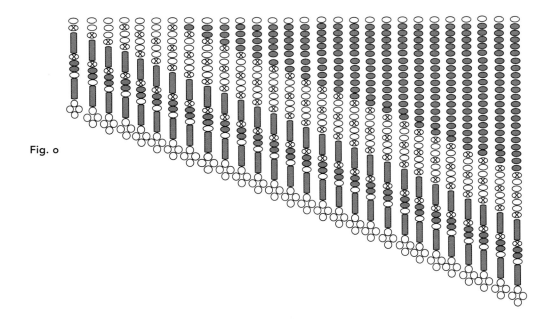

Fig. o

11 When the fringe is completed, turn the work over once more to add the final edging of 40 gold rocailles to the remaining row of bugles.

12 When you reach the last bugle, you will have one thread protruding from one end and two threads from the other. Work the last two as a single thread.

13 The second half of the necklace closure is formed by beading the upper and lower threads as shown in **Fig. p**, finishing with the 6 mm bead followed by a gold rocaille.

15 Make an over hand knot close to this last rocaille, seal with glue and trim away the spare ends.

Fig. p

Fiorata Necklace and Earrings

These are made from black and goldstone glass 'fiorata' beads, rose-coloured crystal which echo the rose on the black beads and 'antique' gold-coated rocailles. This necklace has wonderful texture which has been achieved by mixing three different types of surfaces – smooth, knobbly and sharp. The tools you will need for the necklace are glue, snipe-nosed pliers and scissors; for the earrings, you will need round-nosed pliers, wire cutters and two-part epoxy resin glue for the bouton attachment.

Fig. a

Necklace

Materials

12 black fiorata cylinder beads

13 black fiorata oval beads

26 x 8 mm black fiorata round bead

52 x 4 mm rose-coloured crystal glass beads

1 pack dull gold-coated size 8/0 rocailles

2 calottes

Boat-shaped box clasp

2.5 m approx. medium thickness polyester thread, used doubled

Needle/wire bead threader

Instructions

Before you start threading lay all the beads out following the pattern shown in **Fig. a**. Start at the centre with an oval bead with a rocaille either side, and work upwards to left and right, matching the beads as you go. It is important to balance the threading in this way because the fiorata beads are hand made and differ in size.

1 Thread the needle with the polyester and make a knot at the end of the double strand. Seal with glue and fix a calotte over it. (NB If you are using clamshell calottes, thread them on before you make the knot.)
2 Thread on all the beads following the diagram closely.
3 Pull the thread taut and finish with a knot and calotte.
4 Trim away the surplus threads and attach the calottes to the clasp.

Earrings

Materials

2 black fiorata boutons (with flat back)

2 oval or drop black fiorata beads

2 x 4 mm rose-crystal beads

6 dull gold-coated rocailles

1 pair flat front earfittings with loop

1 pair gold-plated headpins

Instructions

If preferred, omit the upper part of the earrings, with the glass bouton and flat clip, and simply hang the lower threaded headpins from a pair of earhooks.

1 Trim the two pieces of fabric and glue to the earfittings. Allow them to dry thoroughly.

Fig. b

2 Glue the boutons to the earfittings. Again, allow them to dry thoroughly (see **Fig. b**).
3 Thread a headpin with the beads, following the pattern in **Fig. c**.
4 Cut to the appropriate length, allowing about 8 mm spare to make into a neat loop with round-nosed pliers.
5 Hang the threaded pin from the loop of the earfittings and close securely (see **Fig. d**).
6 Make the second earring in the same way.

Fig. c

Fig. d

Scarabee Necklace and Earrings

These are made from size 8/0 silver-lined, rainbow-coated rocailles in a beetle-green colour with a few gold-coated rocailles for extra lustre. The strings of rocailles are attached to the rings of the hanging spacers with calottes; the rows of beads in the necklace are attached in pairs, and to ensure that these lie flat, each pair is linked to the spacer rings with the help of two jump rings, one round and one oval. The upper strings are worked to form a multiple loop and bead closure so that the necklace length may be easily adjusted. If you cannot find round spacer rings like these, use wire circles with a loop at the top; hang the calottes of the beaded strands directly onto them, spacing with beads to prevent bunching. For both necklace and earrings you will need snipe-nosed pliers, scissors, glue and a tape measure.

Fig. a

Necklace

Materials

70 gms rocailles size 8/0, silver-lined green with iridescent coating

5 gms rocailles size 8/0 dull gold coated

2 x 7-ringed pendant hangers (gold finish)

30 calottes (gold finish), preferably clamshell

14 rocailles size 11/0 (to help tighten knots, if using clamshell calottes)

16 oval jump rings (4 mm x 5 mm)

16 round jump rings (5 mm)

1 x 10 mm bead (gold finish)

12 m. approx. fine, strong thread used doubled

1 fine beading needle (split 'big eye' needle)

or rocailles threader with long, curved needle

Instructions

Mix the green and gold rocailles together in a random manner and begin to bead on a doubled strand of thread, allowing an extra 6 cm either end of each row for making the knots. There are fourteen rows in the lower part of the necklace, each of which start and finish with a calotte. Measure each row as you work, adding or removing beads as necessary, and take care to keep the rows in the correct order.

The lengths of the rows are as follows:

Row 1	23 cm	(9")
Row 2	24.5 cm	(9 5/8")
Row 3	25 cm	(9 7/8")
Row 4	25.5 cm	(10")
Row 5	26 cm	(10 1/4")
Row 6	26.5 cm	(10 3/8")
Row 7	27.5 cm	(10 7/8")
Row 8	28 cm	(11")
Row 9	29 cm	(11 3/8")
Row 10	30 cm	(11 3/4")
Row 11	31 cm	(12 1/4")
Row 12	32 cm	(12 5/8")
Row 13	32.5 cm	(12 3/4")
Row 14	33.5 cm	(13 1/8")

1 Starting with Row 1, thread the needle, make a substantial knot at the end and seal with glue.

2 Fix a calotte over this knot, the loop pointing away from the bead thread (see **Fig. b**).

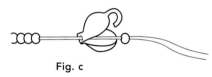

Fig. b

3 Thread on 23 cm (9") of beads.

4 Finish with a calotte. (NB If using a clamshell calotte: thread on the calotte, followed by a size 11/0 rocaille (see **Fig. c**); tie an overhand knot close to the bead, seal the knot with glue, close up the calotte with pliers and trim off the spare threads.)

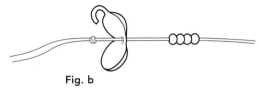

Fig. c

5 Repeat this process for the remaining thirteen rows.

6 Hook the beginning calottes of Rows 1 and 2 into a round jump ring and close up the loops (see **Fig. d**).

7 Open an oval jump ring by twisting gently sideways and use it to link the round jump ring to the first loop of the pendant hanger (see **Fig. e**).

8 Repeat the process at the other end.

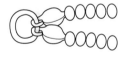

Fig. d

Fig. e

9 The remaining rows of beads are attached in pairs in the same way (Steps 6-8).

The upper strands of the necklace form an adjustable loop and bead closure; these are worked as follows:

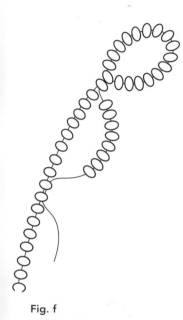

Fig. f

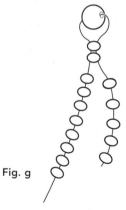

Fig. g

Right-hand upper strand

1 Use a doubled strand of thread, tie a slip knot and thread on a calotte (do not close up yet).
2 Thread on 53 rocailles.
3 Coil the thread back and form a loop of 16 rocailles, by passing the needle through 2 rocailles previously threaded (see **Fig. f**: a single thread is shown to avoid confusion).
4 Add 8 rocailles, and form a second loop by counting 8 rocailles of the previously threaded strand and taking the needle through the next 2 rocailles.
5 Repeat Step 4 once again.
6 Add 12 rocailles.
7 Take the needle through the remaining three rocailles of the first strand.
8 Carefully undo the first slip knot and pass these threads through a clamshell calotte followed by the needle end.
9 Join all the threads together, pull taut and make an overhand knot close inside the calotte.
10 Seal the knot, close up the calotte and trim away spare threads.
11 Link this strand to the top ring of the pendant hanger, using a round and oval jump ring.

Left-hand upper strand

1 To make the left-hand upper string, start off as before but thread on 38 rocailles, followed by the 10 mm bead.
2 Take the thread back through the first 2 rocailles and pull taut, adjusting the large bead so that it is drawn neatly against the rocailles (see **Fig. g**).
3 Add 33 rocailles.
4 Take the thread back through the remaining three rocailles of the first strand and finish in the same way as the right-hand upper string of the necklace.
5 Attach the necklace strand to the other pendant hanger as before.

Earrings

Materials

12 gms rocailles size 8/0 silver-lined green with iridescent coating

1 gm rocailles size 8/0 gold-coated

1 pair ear fittings with hooks

2 x 7-ringed pendant hangers

14 calottes

Instructions

For each earring you need four rows of rocailles, secured with a slip knot at either end. The rows of rocailles decrease in length as follows:

2 x Row 1   12 cm   (4 3/4")
2 x Row 2   10.5 cm   (4 1/8")
2 x Row 3   9 cm   (3 1/2")
2 x Row 4   7.5 cm   (3")

1 Arrange the rows in two sets of four, one set for each earring (the longest row will form the outer loop and the shortest, the middle loop)

2 Undo the slip knots of Rows 1, 2, and 3 and attach a calotte at either end.

3 Take Row 1 and hook the calottes into the outer rings of the pendant hanger to form the outer loop (see **Fig.h**). Close up the hooks of the calottes.

4 Hook the calottes of Row 2 into the neighbouring rings, so that the second loop sits just inside the first.

5 Repeat with Row 3, moving inwards.

6 With Row 4, undo the slip knots, and carefully, so as not to lose any beads, pass one end of thread through the first bead at the other end of the strand, and pull so that the strand curls into a loop (see **Fig.i**).

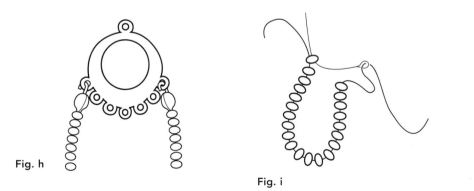

Fig. h

Fig. i

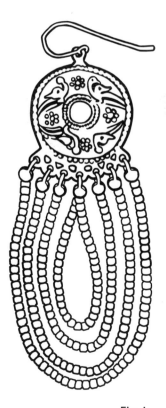

7 Join both threads together, knot and finish with a calotte.

8 The calotte loop is hung from the remaining middle ring of the pendant hanger (see **Fig. j**).

9 Finally, hook an earfitting into the top ring of the pendant hanger.

10 Make the second earring in the same way.

Fig. j

Necklace and Bracelet Lengths

There are standard lengths for necklaces which have special names but when making your own you should adapt these to whichever is the most suitable or flattering to your particular shape.

A Choker   41 cm (16")
B Dog Collar   36 cm (14")
C Collar   41 cm (16")
D Bib   41 cm (16")
E Princess   46 cm (18")
F Matinee   61 cm (24")
G Opera   89 cm (35")
H Rope   112 cm (44")

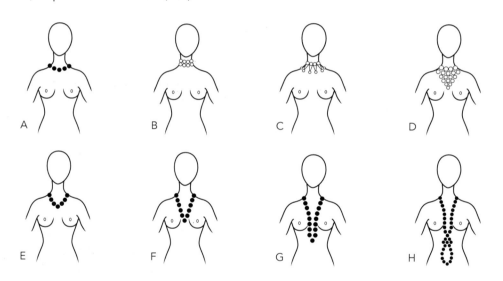

Tip Chokers made with large beads will take up more thread than those with small beads so allow extra.

Bracelet lengths are usually about 18 cm (7") long.

Beads are generally sized in millimetres. When using beads of all the same size, the table below will help to calculate the number necessary for the given lengths.

Length	4 mm	5 mm	6 mm	8 mm	10 mm
40 cm (16")	100	80	67	50	40
45 cm (18")	112	90	75	56	45
66 cm (26")	165	132	110	82	66
90 cm (36")	225	180	150	112	90

Bibliography and Further Reading

Some of the following publications are now out of print and are only available in reference libraries.

Allen, Jamey D. 'Cane Manufacture for Mosaic Glass Beads', *Ornament 5, 7, nos. 4 & 1*, 1982; 'Chevron – Star – Rosetta Beads', *Ornament 7, nos. 1-4*, 1983-4

Beck, Horace C. 'The Classification and Nomenclature of Beads and Pendants', *The London Society of Antiquaries, Archaeologia LXXVII*, 1927; 'Beads from Taxila', *India: Archaeological Survey Memoirs*, 1939-41;'The Magical Properties of Beads', *The Bead Journal 2, no. 4*, 1976

Cole, Herbert M. 'Artistic and Communicative Values of Beads in Kenya and Ghana', *The Bead Journal 1, no. 3*, 1975

Delaroziere, Marguerite F. 'Mauritanian Beads', *Ornament 8, no. 3*, 1985

Dubin, Lois Sherr *The History of Beads*, Thames and Hudson, 1987

Erikson, Joan Mowatt *The Universal Bead*, W.W. Norton, 1969

Fisher, Angela *Africa Adorned*, Collins, 1984

Francis, Peter Jnr. 'A Handbook of Bead Materials', *The World of Beads Monograph, Series 5*, Lapis Route Books, 1982; 'The Glass Beads of India', *The World of Beads Monograph, Series 7*, Lapis Route Books, 1982; 'The Bead Dictionary', *The World of Beads Monograph, Series 9*, Lapis Route Books, 1989; 'The Historical Import of Beads', *Bead Journal 3, no. 3*; 'Bead Report VI: The Earliest Beads in India', *Ornament 5, 6, nos. 4 & 1*, 1982; 'Bead Report VII: When India was Bead Maker to the World', *Ornament 6, no. 2*, 1982; 'Bead Report VIII: Minor Indian Bead Makers', *Ornament 6, no. 3*, 1983; 'Bead Report IX: Bangles and Beads', *Ornament 6, no. 4*, 1983

Gold Filled Manufacturers Association *The Gold Filled Story*, 1982

Guido, Margaret 'The Glass Beads of the Prehistoric and Roman Periods in Britain and Ireland', *The London Society of Antiquarians, no. 35*, 1978

Harris, Elizabeth *A Bead Primer*, The Bead Museum, 1987

Karklins, Karlis *Glass Beads*, Natural Historic Parks & Sites Branch Parks, Canada, 1982

Kennedy, Sylvia S.J. & Liu, R.K. 'Contemporary Cane Beadmaking', *Ornament 8, no. 3*, 1985

Kidd, Kenneth E. *Glass Beadmaking from the Middle Ages to the Early 19th Century*, Natural Historic Parks & Sites Branch Parks, Canada, 1979

King, C.W. *The Natural History of Precious Stones and of the Precious Metals*, Bell & Daldy, 1870; *Antique Gems, Their Origin, Uses and Value*, 1860; *The Natural History, Ancient and Modern, of Precious Stones and Gems*, 1865; 'Antique Gems', *Edinburgh Revue 254 Oct.*, 1866

Kunz, G.F. *The Curious Lore of Precious Stones*, Halcyon House, 1913; *The Magic of Jewels and Charms*, 1915

Liu Robert K. 'Glass Mosaic or Millefiori & Face Beads', *Bead Journal 1, no. 1*, 1974; 'Chinese Cloisonne and Enamel Beads', *Bead Journal 1, no. 1*, 1974; 'Mould Made Glass African Beads', *Bead Journal 1, no. 2*, 1974; 'Ancient Chinese Glass Beads', *Bead Journal 2, no. 2*, 1975; 'Early 20th Century Bead Catalogues', *Bead Journal 2, no. 2*, 1975; 'Molded and Interlocking Glass beads', *Bead Journal 2, no. 3*, 1976

Mack, John (Ed.) *Ethnic Jewellery*, British Museum Publication, 1988
Mason, Anita & Packer, *An Illustrated Dictionary of Jewellery*, Osprey, 1973

Newman, Harold *An Illustrated Dictionary of Jewelry*, Thames and Hudson, 1981

Ogden, Jack *Jewellery of the Ancient World*, Trefoil Books, 1982

Oved, Sah *The Book of Necklaces*, Arthur Barker, 1953

Powell, Harold *The Pottery Handbook of Clay, Glaze and Colour*, 1968

Picard, John & Ruth 'Chevron Beads from the West African Trade', *Vol 1, Picard African Imports*, 1986; 'Tabular Beads from the West African Trade', *Vol 2*, 1986; 'Fancy Beads from the West African Trade', *Vol 3*, 1987; 'White Hearts, Feather and Eye Beads from the West African Trade', *Vol 4*, 1988; 'Russian Blues, Faceted and Fancy Beads from the West African Trade', *Vol 5*, 1989; 'Millefiori Beads from the West African Trade', *Vol 6*, 1991; 'Chevron and Nueva Cadiz Beads', *Vol 7*, 1992

Reeve, Lynn from *The Craft of the Potter* (ed. Michael Casson and Anna Jackson), BBC TV Advisory Committee, 1976

Schuler, F. & L. *Glassforming*, 1971

Schuler, F. *Flame working*

Seligman, C.G. & Beck, H. *Far Eastern Glass: Some Western Origins*, 1938

Seyd, Mary *Introducing Beads*, Batsford, 1973

van der Sleen, W.G.N. 'Ancient Glass Beads, with special reference to the beads of East and Central Africa and the Indian Ocean', *Journal of the Royal Anthropological Institute of Great Britain & Northern Ireland*, 1958; *A Handbook on Beads*, Musée du Verre, 1973

Streeter, Edwin W. *Precious Stones and Gems*, George Bell & Sons, 1898

Weyl, W.A. *Coloured Glasses*

Wilkins, Eithne *The Rose Garden Game: The Symbolic Background to the European Prayer Beads*, Victor Gollanz 1969

Wolverhampton Polytechnic 'Plastics Antiques', *Catalogue 1850s to 1950s B.I.P.L.*, 1977

List of Suppliers

United Kingdom
The Bead Shop
43 Neal Street
London WC2H 9PJ

Beads
259 Portobello Road
London W11 1LR

Creative Beadcraft
20 Beak Street
London W1R 3HA

Hobby Horse
15 Langton Street
London SW10 OJL

London Bead Company
25 Chalk Farm Road
London NW1 8AG

Janet Coles Bead Emporium
128 Notting Hill Gate
London W11 3QG

Janet Coles Beads Ltd.*
Perdiswell Cottage
Bilford Road
Worcester WR3 3QA

Exchange Findings
11 Hatton Wall
London
EC1N 8FH

Bill and Martin Tufnell (glass beads)
Unit 8
EYBC Units
Kellythorpe Industrial Estate
Kellythorpe
Driffield
YO25 9DJ

The Brighton Bead Shop
21 Sydney Street
Brighton
East Sussex BN1 4EN

Spangles*
1 Casburn Lane
Burwell
Cambridge CB5 OED

The Rocking Rabbit
135 Cambridge Road
Milton
Cambridge CB4 6BD

The Northern Bead Company
The Corn Exchange
Call Lane
Leeds LS1 7BR

For further information, please send a
SAE to:
The Bead Society of Great Britain
Carole Morris (Secretary)
1 Casburn Lane
Burwell
Cambridgeshire CB5 OED

United States of America

Beadworks
139 Washington Street
South Norwalk CT 06854

Beadworks
905 South Ann Street
Baltimore MD 21231

Beadworks
23 Church Street
Cambridge MA 02318

Beadworks
1420 Avenue K
Plano
Dallas TX 75074

Beadworks
68 Greenwich Avenue
Greenwich CT 06830

Art to Wear
4202 Water Oaks Lane
Tampa FL 33624

Brahm Ltd
PO Box 1
Lake Charles LA 70602

The Garden of Beading
PO Box 1535
Redway CA 95560

Ornamental Resources Inc.
PO Box 3010
Idaho Springs CO 80452

Helby Import Company
74 Rupert Avenue
Staten Island
New York NY 10314

For further information, please contact:
The Bead Society of Greater New York
236 West 27 Street
Room 590
New York NY 10001

The Bead Society
PO Box 2513
Culver City
California CA 90231

The Bead Society of Greater Washington
PO Box 70036
Chevy Chase MD 208/3 - 0036

Center for the Study of Beadwork
PO Box 13719
Portland OR 97213

Australia

Worldwide Beads
PO Box 40
Teesdale
Victoria 3328

Pots 'n' Stitches
113 London Circuit
Canberra City 2601

Bead Company
Civic Arcade
405 Victoria Avenue
Chatswood 2067

Yee's Hobbies and Craft
19A Bishop Street
Stuart Park 0820

Beads & Beads
Myer Centre
Queen Street Mall
Brisbane 4000

No Worries Beads & Buttons
Lacey Drive
Aldina 5173

Bead Compnay
216 Liverpool Street
Hobart 7000

Bead Company
336 Smith Street
Collingwood 3066

Creative Bead Imports
255 South Terrace
Fremantle 6162

Canada
Beadworks
126 W. 3rd Avenue
Vancouver
British Columbia
V5Y 1E9

Beadworks
10324-82 Avenue
Edmonton
Alberta
T6E 1Z8

Beads and Plenty More
Ste. 113-755 N.W.
Calgary
Alberta
T2J 0N3

Pacific Western Crafts
Box 40024
Victoria
British Columbia
U8W 3N3

Bead Box
1234 Robson Street
Vancouver
British Columbia
V6E 1C1

Bead Works
103-733 Broadway Avenue
Saskatoon
Saskatchewan
S7N 1B3

New Zealand
The Embroiderer
132 Hinemoa Street
Birkenhead
Auckland

Broomfields
211 Papanui Road
Merivale
Christchurch

Bead Gallery
116 Vanguard St
Nelson
South Island

* Mail order only

Index